# EAK
# THE
# LANGUAGE
# BARRIER!

## Improve Your English
## and Improve Your Life

# BREAK the LANGUAGE BARRIER!
## Improve Your English and Improve Your Life

Carl W. Hart

ISBN-13: 978-0-578-59448-4

# Riverwoods Press
info@riverwoodspress.com

# TABLE OF CONTENTS

## 2.6 Problems with Pronunciation / 80

## 3 · PROBLEMS WITH PUNCTUATION / 85

## ANSWER KEY / 97

**B**ad English is like bad breath—when people notice it, they're too polite to tell you about it. In *Break the Language Barrier!*, I'm not polite. In plain language, I tell you what's wrong and how to get it right.

Why is good English important? Because like it or not, every time you open your mouth to say anything, you are judged. From the way you speak or write, the listener or reader decides things about your education, your intelligence, your social level or your suitability as an employee or romantic partner. Maybe it's not fair, but that's life. Make a mistake in your English, and without even knowing it, you might be branded as someone who is not right for a new job, not right for a promotion, not someone whose thoughts and opinions are worth considering or not someone suitable for a romantic or social relationship. The person you're talking to may keep smiling, but now there's an invisible barrier between you and professional or social advancement.

In today's competitive job market, job seekers need all the help they can get. But using poor English in a job interview can ruin your chances for a job. One of the biggest problems employers have at the white-collar level, in particular among employees involved with corporate communications or dealing with customers, is poor English. Good English can give you the edge you need to beat out the competition for a new job or promotion.

In this book I focus on grammar, word and phrase usage, spelling, punctuation and pronunciation. I also dispel some myths regarding English—things that many people believe that just aren't true. And to help you make fast progress, I've marked the problem areas that are especially important with "WARNING!!!" Pay special attention to these.

Throughout this book I make frequent reference to the Grammar Police. There is no such thing, of course, but if there were, I'd be a good candidate for the Chief of the Grammar Police. It's a convenient way of referring to people who know what is right and notice when you get it wrong. Some, though they might notice, will be inclined to give you a pass, but many will not. They likely won't say anything, but they'll make unkind judgments about you—at the very least that you're not very bright or well-educated—and possibly, depending on where they fit into your life, make judgments that erect an invisible barrier between you and where you want to be professionally, socially or romantically.

If you think your English needs improvement, I commend you for admitting it to yourself and making an effort to do something about it. If this book helps you to improve your English, I'll take the credit. If improving your English helps you get a bigger slice of the pie of life, the credit goes to you.

Carl W. Hart

*carl@carlwhart.com*

# I • PROBLEMS WITH GRAMMAR AND SENTENCES

## 1.1 • Problems with *Be*

### 1.1.1 Not using *be* at all
WARNING!!! This is pretty basic. If you're doing this, you need to stop right now!

| | |
|---|---|
| wrong: | *I sick.* |
| right: | *I <u>am</u> sick.* |
| wrong: | *You crazy.* |
| right: | *You <u>are</u> crazy.* |
| wrong: | *He a doctor.* |
| right: | *He <u>is</u> a doctor.* |
| wrong: | *We late.* |
| right: | *We <u>are</u> late.* |
| wrong: | *They at the supermarket.* |
| right: | *They <u>are</u> at the supermarket.* |

### 1.1.2 Using only *be*
WARNING!!! This is pretty basic too. If you're doing this, you need to stop right now!

| | |
|---|---|
| wrong: | *I <u>be</u> sick.* |
| right: | *I <u>am</u> sick.* |
| wrong: | *You <u>be</u> crazy.* |
| right: | *You <u>are</u> crazy.* |
| wrong: | *He <u>be</u> a doctor.* |
| right: | *He <u>is</u> a doctor.* |
| wrong: | *They <u>be</u> at the supermarket.* |
| right: | *They <u>are</u> at the supermarket.* |

### Quiz 1.1.1 & 1.1.2
Each of these sentences has an error. Find it and correct it.

1. They be in the garage.

2. My sister crazy.

3. She be really angry.

4. Tom and Bob at the beach.

5. Her husband a pilot.

### 1.1.3 Using the wrong past form of *be*

WARNING!!! Another crime against the English language—using the wrong past form of *be*. This is a matter of basic literacy. In case you're not sure, this is what it boils down to:

**past forms of *be***
*I was*
*You were*
*He was*
*She was*
*It was*
*We were*
*They were*

Anything else is just plain wrong.

wrong:  *We <u>was</u> late.*
right:  *We <u>were</u> late.*

wrong:  *They <u>was</u> working.*
right:  *They <u>were</u> working.*

## Quiz 1.1.3
Each of these sentences has an error. Find it and correct it.

1. They was going to the mall.

2. Mary and I was really tired after working all day.

3. Was you at the party last night?

4. When was you at the mall?

5. The students wasn't listening to the teacher.

### 1.1.4 *if I was* or *if I were*?

In the very best English, when talking about things that are impossible (or very unlikely), not real or imaginary, it is better to always use *were* instead of *was*—even with *I, he, she* and *it*. (Don't ask why! It's complicated. Just trust me.)

But using *was* with *I, he, she* and *it* is so common that some (but not all!) members of the Grammar Police consider this a lost cause and are reluctantly willing to give it a pass. However, if you want to speak the very best English, try to remember this. (And when I say *I, he, she* and *it*, I also mean the name of any single person or thing.)

sort of OK:  *If I <u>was</u> rich, I would travel around the world.*
better:  *If I <u>were</u> rich, I would travel around the world.*

sort of OK:  *If she <u>was</u> here, she could answer your question.*
better:  *If she <u>were</u> here, she could answer your question.*

| sort of OK: | *If your father <u>was</u> still alive, he'd be very angry with you.* |
| better: | *If your father <u>were</u> still alive, he'd be very angry with you.* |

| sort of OK: | *Today's Friday. If it <u>was</u> Saturday, I'd be playing golf right now.* |
| better: | *Today's Friday. If it <u>were</u> Saturday, I'd be playing golf right now.* |

But when we're talking about something that really is possible, that is not imaginary, that might be real, *was* is correct.

| correct: | *Larry wasn't at work yesterday. Maybe he was sick. If he <u>was</u> sick, I hope he went to the doctor.* |
| correct: | *Maria said she was going to the party last night, but if she <u>was</u> there, I didn't see her.* |

## Quiz 1.1.4
These sentences aren't totally wrong, but they can be improved.

1. If she was the boss, what do you think she would change around here?

2. I wouldn't do that if I was you.

3. What would you tell him if he was here?

4. If I wasn't a teacher, I'd like to be a scientist.

5. I'd give you a ride if my car wasn't in the shop.

### 1.1.5 *I wish I was* or *I wish I were*?
When you *wish* for something, it's always because it's impossible (or unlikely), not real or imaginary. For that reason, as we saw above, it's always better to use *were* than *was*.

Once again, *was* is reluctantly considered sort of acceptable by some members of the Grammar Police, but if you want to speak the very best English, use *were*.

| sort of OK: | *I wish I <u>was</u> rich.* |
| better: | *I wish I <u>were</u> rich.* |

### 1.1.6 *as if I were* or *as if I was*?
Again, we're talking about something not real, impossible or imaginary.

| sort of OK: | *She talks to me as if I <u>was</u> a servant.* |
| better: | *She talks to me as if I <u>were</u> a servant.* |

| sort of OK: | *He treats me as though I <u>was</u> his son.* |
| better: | *He treats me as though I <u>were</u> his son.* |

This applies to *as though I was/were* as well.

## Quiz 1.1.5 & 1.1.6
These sentences aren't totally wrong, but they can be improved.

1. I wish my son wasn't so lazy.

2. Why do you talk to me as if I was an idiot?

3. Don't you wish today was Friday?

4. My husband acts as though I was invisible.

5. I think he wishes he was single.

# 1.2 • Problems with Pronouns

## 1.2.1 Using the wrong pronoun

Do these sound OK to you?

*Larry and me played tennis yesterday.*
*Sarah and her went to the library.*
*Him and I both like seafood better than anything.*
*When you've finished your test, give it to Prof. Davis or I.*
*The foreman asked Maria and he to work late.*

All of them are wrong, and if any of them sound like something you would say, keep reading because you've probably already been noticed by the Grammar Police.

It boils down to this: *Pronouns* replace nouns (the names of things and people). For example,

with nouns:        *David* ate *the cheeseburger.*
with pronouns:  *He* ate *it.*

In English there are subject pronouns and object pronouns.

**subject pronouns**
*I*
*you*
*he*
*she*
*it*
*we*
*they*

**object pronouns**
*me*
*you*
*him*
*her*
*it*
*us*
*them*

Notice that *you* and *it* are both subject pronouns and object pronouns, so you can't make a mistake with them, but messing up the others, which many people do, is something the Grammar Police can spot a mile away, so it's worth the effort to learn how to use them correctly. It's not that hard.

First of all, you need to get straight on what subjects and objects are. In a basic English sentence, the subject is the doer of the action of the verb, and the object is the receiver of the action of the verb.

These are subjects:

> *They talked to us.*
> *Carlos saw a UFO.*
> *My dog ate my homework.*
> *The jerks who live next door to us threw a bunch of empty beer bottles in our backyard.*

These are objects:

> *They talked to us.*
> *Carlos saw a UFO.*
> *My dog ate my homework.*
> *The jerks who live next door to us threw a bunch of empty beer bottles in our backyard.*

Let's start with this example.

> *Me and Larry played tennis yesterday.*

Now let's forget Larry and assume you played tennis with yourself. Would you say this?

> *Me played tennis yesterday.*

Of course you wouldn't! So why would you use *me* when another pronoun is used? Just remember the handy little trick of trying the sentence without any other nouns or pronouns, and what sounds right will be right. Oh, and remember that in the case of *I*, it always come last.

> wrong:  *Me and Larry played tennis yesterday.*
> right:  *Larry and I played tennis yesterday.*

Let's try the same trick with two more of the examples above.

> *Sarah and her went to the library.*
> *Him and I both like seafood better than anything.*

Would you say this?

> *Her went to the library.*
> *Him likes seafood better than anything.*

Yikes, I hope not, and I don't think you would. Do these sound better?

> *She went to the library.*
> *He likes seafood better than anything.*

They do, don't they? Now you know how to fix these sentences.

> wrong:  *Sarah and her went to the library.*
> right:  *Sarah and she went to the library.*

> wrong:  *Him and I both like seafood better than anything.*
> right:  *He and I both like seafood better than anything.*

Now let's fix the next example.

*When you've finished your test, give it to Prof. Davis or I.*

Which sounds right—*give it to I* or *give it to me*? *Give it to me* sounds right, doesn't it? Now you know what is correct.

wrong:    *When you've finished your test, give it to Prof. Davis or I.*
right:      *When you've finished your test, give it to Prof. Davis or me.*

And if you thought that perhaps *give it to Prof. Davis or myself* might be the answer, think again and see 1.2.4.

Now let's fix the last example.

*The foreman asked Maria and he to work late.*

Which sounds right: *The foreman asked he* or *The foreman asked him*? *The foreman asked him* sounds right, doesn't it? Now you know what is correct.

wrong:    *The foreman asked Maria and he to work late.*
right:      *The foreman asked Maria and him to work late.*

## Quiz 1.2.1
Each of these sentences has an error. Find it and correct it.

1. Me and her went to the mall.

2. Her and her sister speak French.

3. My father is going with my sister and I.

4. Sofia, Rosa, Carlos and me went to a Mexican restaurant.

5. Let's keep this between you and I.

### 1.2.2 *I'm taller than him* or *I'm taller than he*?
Do these sound OK to you?

*She's always been luckier in love than me.*
*Carlos is tall, but I'm taller than him.*
*David can run faster than me.*
*Larry and I would do a better job with this project than them.*
*I speak French better than her.*
*They have a bigger house than us.*

If they do, it means you're making the same mistake that virtually all native speakers do. Here's what it boils down to: Strictly speaking, sentences like these are shortened forms of longer sentences that repeat the verb (or use *do, does* or *did,* substitutes for the verb). Here's what I mean:

*She's always been luckier in love than I've been.*
*Carlos is tall, but I'm taller than he is.*
*David can run faster than I can.*

*Larry and I would do a better job with this project than they would.*
*I speak French better than she does.* (Which really means *I speak French better than she speaks French.*)
*They have a bigger house than we do.* (Which really means *They have a bigger house than we have.*)

All of these sound perfectly OK too, I'm sure you agree, and they are perfectly OK grammarwise. The problem occurs when we save time by not repeating the verb (or not saying *do, does* or *did*). Not repeating the verb or omitting *do, does* or *did* is also perfectly OK, but the result, despite its being perfectly OK, is so uncommon, that to most people it will, ironically, sound wrong even though it isn't. Here's what I mean:

*She's always been luckier in love than I.*
*Carlos is tall, but I'm taller than he.*
*David can run faster than I.*
*Larry and I would do a better job with this project than they.*
*I speak French better than she.*
*They have a bigger house than we.*

I'm pretty sure that the sentences above sound sort of odd to you. They do to me too even though I know they're correct. Right or wrong, if you use this grammar, you'll sound snooty, so my advice is, when you want to use the very best English, use the grammar that repeats the verb or uses *do, does* or *did*. For example, rather than saying

*He's older than me.*
*Sarah makes more money than him.*
*They can play tennis better than us.*

say

*He's older than I am.*
*Sarah makes more money than he does.*
*They can play tennis better than we can.*

## Quiz 1.2.2
Each of these sentences has an error. Find it and correct it.

1. Nobody sings better than her.

2. Do you think Carlos is taller than me?

3. I don't know how anyone could be stupider than him.

4. We have more experience than them.

5. I don't think anyone deserves this award more than us.

### 1.2.3 *It's me* or *It's I*, *It's him* or *It's he*?
This is a rare case where the Grammar Police are lenient. Why? Because saying what is, strictly speaking, wrong is so common that saying what is, strictly speak-

ing, right will sound so odd that people might think you're a weirdo (which you may be). Still, it's a good idea to be aware of this for situations where you need to use the very best English. What it boils down to is that subject pronouns should be used after forms of *be*. I know I've already said that object pronouns should be used after verbs, but *be* is a special case. Trust me.

| wrong but kind of OK: | *It's me.* |
| actually correct: | *It's I.* |

| wrong but kind of OK: | *It was him.* |
| actually correct: | *It was he.* |

I'm a card-carrying member of the Grammar Police, but when I knock on a door, and the person inside asks *Who is it?*, I sure don't say *It is I.* You can if you want people to think you're a weirdo. In informal conversation, most members of the Grammar Police will look the other way at these infractions, but just remember what's right when you need to use the very best English.

## 1.2.4 Problems with *myself* and *yourself*
Do these sound OK to you?

*Bob Smith and myself were transferred to the Seattle office.*
*Mr. Fowler went over last month's sales figures with Johnson and myself.*
*Myself and my wife went to Hawaii last month.*
*I want Bob and yourself to put a cover sheet on the TPS report.*
*I look forward to meeting Ms. Taylor and yourself.*

They're all wrong, so if they sound OK to you, you might be a white-collar windbag. This unnecessary and incorrect use of the reflexive pronouns *myself* and *yourself* is extremely common among people trying to sound important by using bloated language when plain, simple (and correct) language will do. To members of the Grammar Police, they're like fingernails on chalkboard. Fortunately, it's very easy to fix. Here's the secret: If replacing *yourself* with *you* or replacing *myself* with either the subject pronoun *I* or the object pronoun *me* (you do know the difference, don't you?) sounds OK, then that's exactly what you should be using instead of *yourself* or *myself*. Let's try it.

| replace *myself* with *I*: | *Bob Smith and myself were transferred to the Seattle office.* |
| sounds OK and is therefore correct: | *Bob Smith and I were transferred to the Seattle office.* |

| replace *myself* with *me*: | *Mr. Fowler went over last month's sales figures with Johnson and myself.* |
| sounds OK and is therefore correct: | *Mr. Fowler went over last month's sales figures with Johnson and me.* |

replace *myself* with *I*:         *Myself and my wife went to Hawaii last month.*
sounds OK and is therefore correct (with the pronouns switched):
        *My wife and I went to Hawaii last month.*

| replace *yourself* with *you*: | *I want Bob and <u>yourself</u> to put a cover sheet on the TPS report.* |
| sounds OK and is therefore correct: | *I want Bob and <u>you</u> to put a cover sheet on the TPS report.* |
| replace *yourself* with *you*: | *I look forward to meeting John and <u>yourself</u>.* |
| sounds OK and is therefore correct: | *I look forward to meeting John and <u>you</u>.* |

Don't get the idea that *myself* and *yourself* are always wrong. Try replacing them with *I, me* or *you* in these sentences.

*I was alone, so I had to change the tire myself.*
*Do you live by yourself?*
*I shot myself in the foot.*
*You have to complete the test yourself. No one can help you.*

You can't, can you? That means there's nothing wrong with these.

## Quiz 1.2.4

Each of these sentences has one or more errors. Find them and correct them.

1. Myself and John worked on the project together.

2. After the class, I need to talk to Sarah and yourself.

3. You may turn in your report to Prof. Davis or myself.

4. Frank and myself will contact either Maria or yourself after we arrive.

5. Do you want to come with Ali and myself?

## 1.2.5 Problems with *they, them, their* and *themselves*

Do these sentences sound OK to you?

*Someone left their book in the classroom.*
*If a student has a problem, they can talk to their teacher.*
*A call for me? Tell them I'll call them back later.*
*Each student has to do all the work themselves. No one can help them.*

If these sound OK to you, then you're in the habit of solving a defect in the English language the same way that most people do (even some members of the Grammar Police). Normally, using proper English is a simple matter of learning what is wrong and what is right, but here we've come to a problem for which there is no simple solution, or at least no solution that won't make you sound like a goofball (which you may be).

What's the problem? *They, them, their* and *themselves* are plural pronouns, and in each of the examples above, we're talking about one person. Using a plural pronoun, strictly speaking, is a violation of the rules of grammar. So why not use the singular pronouns *he, she, him, her, his, her, himself* and *herself*? We could, but because in each case we don't know if we're talking about a single male or a single female, we'd have to use neutral singular pronouns—if only there were any, but there isn't. That's the defect in the English language I mentioned: There are no neutral singular pronouns. For that reason, some people resort to using both male and female pronouns.

singular pronouns: *Someone left <u>his or her</u> book in the classroom.*
singular pronouns: *If a student has a problem, <u>he or she</u> can talk to <u>his or her</u> teacher.*
singular pronouns: *A call for me? Tell <u>him or her</u> I'll call <u>him or her</u> back later.*
singular pronouns: *Each student has to do all the work <u>himself or herself</u>. No one can help <u>him or her</u>.*

This works, but in everyday speech and writing, it's awfully cumbersome and stuffy. That's why people use plural pronouns as a workaround.

plural pronoun: *Someone left <u>their</u> book in the classroom.*
plural pronoun: *If a student has a problem, <u>they</u> can talk to <u>their</u> teacher.*
plural pronoun: *A call for me? Tell <u>them</u> I'll call <u>them</u> back later.*
plural pronoun: *Each student has to do all the work <u>themselves</u>. No one can help <u>them</u>.*

These sound natural and not cumbersome and stuffy, I'm sure you agree, but grammarwise, they're just plain wrong. What to do? Here's my advice: Go ahead and use plural pronouns in casual conversation and writing. The Grammar Police may frown, but they'll generally look the other way. In careful writing, however, when you need to use the very best English, use both pronouns. If it's just here and there, it won't sound so cumbersome and stuffy. Or you can do what I often do— if possible, rewrite the sentence to avoid the problem. The easiest way is to rewrite it so that it's plural.

*If any students have a problem, they can talk to their teachers.*
*The students have to do all the work themselves. No one can help them.*

And one last thing, do not, under any circumstances, use the ghastly mutant words *themself, theirselves* or *theirself*. There are no such words. That's where the Grammar Police draw the line.

## Quiz 1.2.5

These would be sort of OK in casual speech, but not in the very best, formal English. Rewrite them so that they would not make the Grammar Police look at you funny. There is more than one solution for some.

1. [In a school for girls.] Who didn't finish their homework?

2. When someone calls in sick, they have to bring a doctor's note.

3. If I knew who stole my bike, I'd punch them in the face.

4. If a student loses their ID, they have to talk to the principal.

5. Each girl must complete the assignment themself. No one can help them.

### 1.2.6 *could of, should of, would of* or *could have, should have, would have*?

WARNING!!! *Could of, should of* and *would of* are never correct. *Could have, should have* and *would have* (sometimes contracted to *could've, should've* and *would've*) are always correct. It's that simple.

wrong:   *could of, should of* and *would of*
right:    *could have, should have* and *would have*

### 1.2.7 *it's* or *its*?

Do these look OK to you?

*It's been raining for three hours.*
*The plane crashed after it's wing fell off.*
*I tried to fix it, but it's still broken.*
*A leopard can't change it's spots.*

Here's a hint: Two of them are OK; two aren't.

Give up? These two are OK,

*It's been raining for three hours.*
*I tried to fix it, but it's still broken.*

and these two are not.

*The plane crashed after it's wing fell off.*
*A leopard can't change it's spots.*

Do you see the difference? In the first two examples, *it's* is a contraction of either *it has* or *it is*. But in the second two, can *it's* be replaced with either *it has* or *it is*? Nope. In both cases, *it's* should be *its*, without an apostrophe. *Its* is what's called a possessive adjective. Possessive adjectives show, you guessed it, possession.

**possessive adjectives**
*my*
*your*
*his*
*her*
*its*
*our*
*their*

Do you see any apostrophes? No, you don't. The reason people get confused is that possessive *nouns* do require apostrophes.

*My cat's name is Larry.*
*Mary's car won't start.*
*These are my books, and those are David's.*

This might seem like a punctuation problem—another example of unnecessary, incorrect apostrophes, something we'll discuss later and something the Grammar

Police are always on the alert for—but it's really more of a grammar thing: knowing the difference between possessive adjectives and possessive nouns. And now you do!

## Quiz 1.2.7

Each of these sentences has one or more errors. Find them and correct them.

1. It's a beautiful house, but it's roof is in really bad condition.

2. The restaurant raised it's prices.

3. Its well known that you can't judge a book by it's cover.

4. Chicago is known for it's skyline.

5. Its been a long time since it's design was changed.

### 1.2.8 *who* or *whom, whoever* or *whomever*?

Befuddled by *whom*? Afraid to use *whom* for fear of making a mistake? Well, you're not alone, which is why many people just use *who* all the time. This isn't the greatest grammatical sin in the world. The Grammar Police are generally pretty lenient about this, but once again, it's a nice thing to know when you want to use the very best English. Try casually slipping *whom* or *whomever* into a conversation and watch your friends' estimation of you grow before your eyes.

It boils down to this: *Who* and *whoever* are for subjects and *whom* and *whomever* are for objects. The trick to figuring out which to use is to simplify and complete the sentence by plugging either a subject pronoun or an object pronoun into it.

**subject pronouns** (Use *who* or *whoever* for these.)
*I*
*you*
*he*
*she*
*it*
*we*
*they*

**object pronouns** (Use *whom* or *whomever* for these.)
*me*
*you*
*him*
*her*
*it*
*us*
*them*

Let's try it. Would you use *who* or *whom* for this sentence?

*I haven't seen the man (who/whom) you're looking for.*

Here's the trick: First, simplify the sentence by focusing on the verb.

*you're <u>looking</u> for*

Now complete it with *he* or *him*—whichever sounds right.

*you're looking for <u>him</u>*

*Him* sounds right, and that means *whom* is what you need.

*I haven't seen the man <u>whom</u> you're looking for.*

Let's try some more.

*The FBI agents know (who/whom) put the bomb in the potato salad.*
simplify:                               *put the bomb in the potato salad*
subject pronoun *she* sounds right:    *<u>she</u> put the bomb in the potato salad*
use *who*:                         *The FBI agents know <u>who</u> put the bomb in the potato salad.*

*(Whoever/Whomever) did this is in big trouble.*
simplify:                               *did this*
subject pronoun *he* sounds right:    *<u>he</u> did this*
use *whoever*:                      *<u>Whoever</u> did this is in big trouble.*

*The promotion will be given to (whoever/whomever) you choose.*
simplify:                               *given to*
object pronoun *him* sounds right:    *given to <u>him</u>*
use *whomever*:                   *The promotion will be given to <u>whomever</u> you choose.*

But there is a time when you must use *whom*. It's when *whom* follows a preposition (words like *to, from, on, under, next to, of, about* and *with*). For example,

*<u>To whom</u> are you speaking?*
*A man <u>with whom</u> I work is from Germany.*
*The people <u>next to whom</u> we live make a lot of noise.*
*<u>About whom</u> are you speaking?*

## Quiz 1.2.8
Circle the word that correctly completes the sentence.

   1. (Who/Whom) do you think is the best candidate?

   2. Tell me (who/whom) you're going to the party with.

   3. I'll vote for (whoever/whomever) I think will lower taxes.

   4. Jennifer Birch is the woman (who/whom) the company promoted.

   5. Jennifer Birch is the woman (who/whom) was promoted by the company.

## 1.2.9 *these kind of* or *these kinds of*?
Would you say *Those child are cute* or *These shoe aren't comfortable*? Of course not.

But would you say *I hate those kind of people* or *These kind of apples are delicious?* Odds are you would because many people do, but don't! What it boils down to is very simple: If you're using *these* or *those*, *kind* should be plural: *kinds.*

wrong:   *these <u>kind</u>, those <u>kind</u>*
right:    *these <u>kinds</u>, those <u>kinds</u>*

The same goes for *sort* and *type*: *these sorts* or *those sorts*, *these types* or *those types.*

## Quiz 1.2.9
Each of these sentences has an error. Find it and correct it.

1. These kind of problems make me really angry.

2. Do you like those kind of cookies?

3. I told my daughter to stay away from those type of guys.

4. He loves to read these sort of books.

5. I don't like being around these kind of dogs.

## 1.2.10 *The boss is angry about me being late* or *The boss is angry about my being late?*
Here's a way to dazzle your friends and co-workers and earn points with the Grammar Police. It's a little-known fact that in the very best English, possessive adjectives and possessive nouns should be used with gerunds. Huh? OK, first of all, this is what possessive adjectives and possessive nouns are.

possessive adjective:   *This is <u>my</u> book.*
possessive noun:      *This is <u>Mary's</u> book.*

And second, here is what a gerund is: a verb in the *ing* form that's used as a noun.

*I hate <u>waking up</u> early.*
*<u>Learning</u> Japanese is hard work.*

Sometimes we want to identify a certain person with a gerund. Most people use object pronouns

*My husband is worried about <u>me</u> drinking so much.*
*<u>Him</u> being late to the meeting really made the boss angry.*
*I appreciate <u>you</u> taking me to the airport.*

or proper nouns,

*Do you recall <u>Larry</u> telling you not to do that again?*

and usually that will work, but it's not the very best English. Why? Remember, a gerund is a noun, and that means it can be replaced with a noun that is not a gerund. For example, in these sentences, the gerund *dancing* can be replaced with *chocolate* and the sentence still makes sense.

*I like <u>dancing</u>.*

*I like <u>chocolate</u>.*

And that's why it makes sense to use possessive adjectives and possessive nouns with gerunds rather than object pronouns and proper nouns. Let's try this sentence.

*My wife doesn't like <u>me</u> smoking in the house.*

Now let's replace the gerund, *smoking,* with a noun that isn't a gerund.

*My wife doesn't like <u>me</u> friends.*

Sounds awful, doesn't it? But *my* would sound fine with both, wouldn't it?

*My wife doesn't like <u>my</u> smoking in the house.*
*My wife doesn't like <u>my</u> friends.*

That tells you that *my* is not only acceptable; it's preferable.

Here are the other examples above with the object pronouns replaced with possessive adjectives or possessive nouns.

*<u>His</u> being late to the meeting really made the boss angry.*
*I appreciate <u>your</u> taking me to the airport.*
*Do you recall <u>Larry's</u> telling you not to do that again?*

Here are some more examples of possessive adjectives and possessive nouns used with gerunds.

*I resent <u>Michael's</u> being promoted instead of me.*
*What does your wife think about <u>your</u> going sky diving?*
*I'm not happy about <u>my daughter's</u> going out with that loser.*
*I hope you don't mind <u>my</u> asking you something personal.*
*<u>David's</u> calling in sick so much is what got him fired.*
*<u>His</u> leaving the party so early surprised everyone.*
*They regretted <u>our</u> missing the wedding.*

## Quiz 1.2.10

These would be sort of OK in casual speech, but not in the very best, formal English. Rewrite them so that they will impress the Grammar Police.

1. I'm sick and tired of you complaining!

2. I was really shocked at him having quit his job.

3. Mary selling her house and moving to Alaska really surprised me.

4. My wife was furious about me losing the house in a poker game.

5. I hate my son working as a lion tamer.

# 1.3 • Problems with Singular/Plural

## 1.3.1 *there's two* or *there are two*?
Do these sound OK to you?

*There's two people in my office that I can't stand.*
*There's a lot of things that I don't like about both of them.*

I hope not. To the Grammar Police, it sounds really dumb and sloppy. What's the problem? If you take a second to think about it, what is wrong should be obvious. *Is* is singular. *Are* is plural. *Is* would only be correct if there were just one person with one annoying characteristic.

*There's one person in my office that I can't stand.*
*There's one thing that I don't like about him.*

Otherwise, use *are*:

*There are two people in my office that I can't stand.*
*There are a lot of things that I don't like about them.*

Is *there's a lot* ever correct? Yes, if we're talking about something that we don't count (or don't ordinarily count).

*There's too much salt in this soup.*
*There's a lot of snow on the roof.*

And by the way, only *a lot* is correct. There's no such word as *alot*. More on that later. *Lots,* however has the same meaning as *a lot.* They're interchangeable.

## Quiz 1.3.1
Each of these sentences has an error. Find it and correct it.

1. There's three reasons I don't want to do it.

2. David thinks there's aliens on the moon.

3. There's some people waiting to see you.

4. There's a lot of mice living in our kitchen.

5. Do you know if there's 30 days in June or 31?

## 1.3.2 Irregular plurals
Irregular plurals are nouns that don't change from singular to plural in the usual way, by adding *s*. Some of them everyone knows and gets right, like *man/men* and *child/children*.

But there are many more that people frequently mess up. This is something the Grammar Police notice, so pay attention. Often, because it's the form in common use, the irregular plural isn't what causes confusion. It's the less commonly used singular form that the irregular plural form comes from that's the problem. But first of all, let me explain that many of these are words that English has borrowed from other languages—languages which have different ways of changing from singular to plural. English is inconsistent about following those foreign rules. Sometimes adding *s* or using the plural for singular is given a pass by the Grammar Police, but for others, the Grammar Police expect you to get it right and notice when you don't. (Though not all members of the force will agree on some of these—they're like that.) So here goes. You'll see that in some cases, where the Anglicized plural has gained acceptance, I show that as well as the irregular plural. You can use either.

**singular/plural**

### plural ends with *a*
*criterion/criteria*
*phenomenon/phenomena* (A particular pet peeve of mine. If you're an educated know-it-all who's in the habit of discussing *phenomena*, you really ought to get this one right. You won't sound educated if you don't.)

### plural ends with *i* (pronounced like the letter *i*)
*alumnus/alumni*
*cactus/cacti* or *cactuses*
*fungus/fungi*
*nucleus/nuclei*
*radius/radii* or *radiuses*
*stimulus/stimuli*
*syllabus/syllabi*

### plural ends with *ae* (pronounced *ee*)
*alga/algae*
*alumna/alumnae*
*antenna/antennae* or *antennas*
*formula/formulae* or *formulas*
*nebula/nebulae* or *nebulas*
*vertebra/vertebrae* or *vertebras*

### plural ends with *ses* (pronounced *seez*)
*analysis/analyses*
*basis/bases*
*crisis/crises*
*diagnosis/diagnoses*
*ellipsis/ellipses*
*hypothesis/hypotheses*
*neurosis/neuroses*
*oasis/oases*
*parenthesis/parentheses*
*synopsis/synopses*
*thesis/theses*

### plural ends with *ces* (pronounced *seez*)
*appendix/appendices* or *appendixes*
*index/indices* or *indexes*
*vortex/vortices* or *vortexes*

### plural ends with *a*
*addendum/addenda*

*bacterium/bacteria*
*curriculum/curricula*
*datum/data*
*erratum/errata*
*medium/media*
*memorandum/memoranda* or *memorandums*
*millennium/millennia*
*podium/podia* or *podiums*
*referendum/referenda* or *referendums*
*stadium/stadia* or *stadiums*
*stratum/strata*
*symposium/symposia* or *symposiums*
*ultimatum/ultimata* or *ultimatums*

**s added to nouns followed by adjectives (Notice where the s is.)**
*attorney general/attorneys general*
*chief of staff/chiefs of staff*
*court martial/courts martial*

**miscellaneous**
*axis/axes*
*brother-in-law,* etc./*brothers-in-law,* etc.
*corps/corps* (The singular is pronounced KOR. The plural is pronounced KORZ.)
*die/dice*
*man-of-war/men-of-war*
*octopus/octopuses* (*Octopi* is wrong.)
*passerby/passersby*

# Quiz 1.3.2
Each of these sentences has an error. Find it and correct it.

1. The divers were eaten by a group of giant octopi.

2. Both of my brother-in-laws speak Spanish.

3. There were four chief of staffs during the Obama administration.

4. There were two attorney generals during the Obama administration.

5. This phenomena cannot be explained.

## 1.3.3 *either/neither* problems
Do these sound OK to you? If so, keep reading.

*Neither of the stores have my size in stock.*
*Either of the plans are OK.*
*Neither of my kids do any work around the house.*

In each of these sentences, the verbs should be singular.

**BREAK THE LANGUAGE BARRIER!**

*Neither of the stores <u>has</u> my size in stock.*
*Either of the plans <u>is</u> OK.*
*Neither of my kids <u>does</u> any work around the house.*

People get confused when a phrase starting with *of* and containing a plural noun precedes the verb. If you remove it, you'll see that the singular verb sounds right.

plural verb sounds wrong:     *Neither <u>have</u> my size in stock.*
singular verb sounds right:    *Neither <u>has</u> my size in stock.*

plural verb sounds wrong:     *Either <u>are</u> OK.*
singular verb sounds right:    *Either <u>is</u> OK.*

plural verb sounds wrong:     *Neither <u>do</u> any work around the house.*
singular verb sounds right:    *Neither <u>does</u> any work around the house.*

Do these sound OK to you?

*Neither his parents nor his sister like his new wife.*
*Either the twins or Jim are going to be next.*
*If either Mark or Tom are at the party, I'm going to turn around and leave.*

They probably do sound OK to you, but they're not OK. When we have *either…or* or *neither…nor*, the rule is that the verb agrees with the subject closest to the verb. Whether the first subject is singular or plural doesn't matter. It's whether the noun that comes right before the verb is singular or plural that determines whether the verb is singular or plural.

*Neither his parents nor <u>his sister</u> <u>likes</u> his new wife.*
*Either the twins or <u>Jim</u> <u>is</u> going to be next.*
*If either Mark or <u>Tom</u> <u>is</u> at the party, I'm going to turn around and leave.*

## Quiz 1.3.3
Each of these sentences has an error. Find it and correct it.

1. Neither of those bookstores have the book I'm looking for.

2. Either of these routes are OK.

3. Neither of my kids want to come for Christmas dinner.

4. Neither the chief of the police nor the detectives have a clue who did it.

5. If either of your brothers want to come, it's OK with me.

## 1.3.4 *each is* or *each are*?
Does this sound OK to you? If so, keep reading.

*Each of the boys and girls have different needs.*

Singular verbs should be used with *each*.

*Each of the boys and girls <u>has</u> different needs.*

### 1.3.5 *everybody is* or *everybody are?*

Does this sound OK to you?

*Everyone in the class are going to the game.*

I hope not. The indefinite pronouns *everyone, everybody, no one, no body, someone, somebody, anyone* and *anybody* take singular nouns. Although it seems logical to use a plural verb when we're clearly talking about more than one person, especially with *everyone* and *everybody*, singular verbs are correct no matter how large the group.

*Everyone agrees with me.*
*Everybody in this family is nuts.*

And how about these? How do they sound?

*No one did their homework.*
*Everyone in the office thought their Christmas bonus was too small.*

The problem with these has already been discussed, so if you're wondering what's wrong, have a look at 1.2.5.

## Quiz 1.3.4 & 1.3.5

Each of these sentences has an error. Find it and correct it.

1. Everybody that I talked to agree with me.

2. Someone forgot their umbrella.

3. Each of my cats have different personalities.

4. Anyone who believe that is crazy.

5. Each of these pairs of shoes are the wrong size.

### 1.3.6 *none is* or *none are?*

Both are correct. That *none* must be used only with singular verbs is a myth. See 1.8.5.

### 1.3.7 *couple*—singular or plural?

Sometimes people are confused about whether *couple* takes a singular or plural verb. Look at these examples and choose the verb that you think is correct.

*A couple of students (is/are) waiting to talk to me.*
*The couple (is/are) dancing.*
*A couple of my coworkers (eat/eats) lunch at their desks every day.*
*The couple (eat/eats) dinner here every Saturday.*

Hmmm, some sound right with plural verbs and some sound right with singular verbs, right? Yes, that's right. Here are the answers:

*A couple of students are waiting to talk to me.*
*The couple is dancing.*
*A couple of my coworkers eat lunch at their desks every day.*
*The couple eats dinner here every Saturday.*

Here's what it boils down to: *A couple* takes a plural verb but *the couple* takes a singular verb.

## Quiz 1.3.7

Circle the word that correctly completes the sentence.

1. A couple of dogs (was/were) fighting outside.

2. The couple (is/are) going out to dinner.

3. A couple of my friends (go/goes) to Florida every winter.

4. A couple of people (have/has) called about the car I'm selling.

5. The couple (were/was) given the worst seat in the restaurant.

# 1.4 • Problems with Negative Sentences

## 1.4.1 *he doesn't* or *he don't*?

Do these sound OK to you?

*Mary don't know the answer.*
*He don't have any money.*

WARNING!!! If they do, then you'd better hide under the bed because the Grammar Police are looking for you. This is a felony. This really is a matter of basic literacy, so if you're committing this crime against the English language, stop!

Here's what it boils down to: When we're talking about one person (other than yourself) or one thing, we use *does,* not *do.* Don't ask why. Trust me.

*I don't*
*You don't*
*He doesn't*
*She doesn't*
*It doesn't*
*We don't*
*They don't*

And the same goes with questions.

*Don't I*
*Don't you*
*Doesn't he*
*Doesn't she*
*Doesn't it*
*Don't we*
*Don't they*

Remember,

horribly incorrect:   *Mary <u>don't</u> know the answer.*

| | |
|---|---|
| correct: | *Mary <u>doesn't</u> know the answer.* |
| horribly incorrect: | *He <u>don't</u> have any money.* |
| correct: | *He <u>doesn't</u> have any money.* |

## Quiz 1.4.1

Each of these sentences has an error. Find it and correct it.

1. Don't she have beautiful eyes?

2. Jimmy don't like vegetables.

3. I want to go out, but my wife don't.

4. Why don't Carlos like Maria?

5. I think she don't love me anymore.

## 1.4.2 The dreaded double negative

Do these sound OK to you?

*She didn't go nowhere.*
*I don't want nothing to eat.*
*We didn't tell nobody.*

WARNING!!! If so, then yikes! As a member of the Grammar Police, I'm declaring an emergency. This is another matter of basic literacy, a felony that will make people assume some pretty negative things regarding your education and social level. Here's what it boils down to:

In correct English grammar, the rule is only one negative word to a sentence. That gives you two correct options.

| | |
|---|---|
| horribly incorrect: | *She didn't go <u>nowhere</u>.* |
| correct: | *She didn't go <u>anywhere</u>.* |
| correct: | *She went <u>nowhere</u>.* |
| | |
| horribly incorrect: | *I don't want <u>nothing</u> to eat.* |
| correct: | *I don't want <u>anything</u> to eat.* |
| correct: | *I want <u>nothing</u> to eat.* |
| | |
| horribly incorrect: | *We didn't tell <u>nobody</u>.* |
| correct: | *We didn't tell <u>anybody</u>.* |
| correct: | *We told <u>nobody</u>.* |

## Quiz 1.4.2

Each of these sentences has an error. Find it and correct it.

1. I didn't go nowhere yesterday.

2. She doesn't want nothing to eat.

3. Mark doesn't trust nobody.

4. The doctor can't do nothing for him.

5. Didn't you go nowhere last night?

### 1.4.3 When *ain't* is correct and when it ain't
WARNING!!! The rule about when *ain't* is correct is pretty easy to remember: It's NEVER correct. This is another matter of basic literacy, so unless you want people to think you ain't educated, never say *ain't*!

# 1.5 • Problems with Perfect Tenses

### 1.5.1 *if I would have…*
Do these sound OK to you?

> *If I would have known you were coming, I would have baked a cake.*
> *You might not have failed the test if you would have studied for it.*

If they do, then you're making a common mistake. In both cases, the *if*-clause is wrong. *Would have* should be *had*.

wrong:  *If I <u>would have</u> known you were coming, I would have baked a cake.*
right:   *If I <u>had</u> known you were coming, I would have baked a cake.*

wrong:  *You might not have failed the test if you <u>would have</u> studied for it.*
right:   *You might not have failed the test if you <u>had</u> studied for it.*

It might not seem like a big deal, but the Grammar Police notice these things.

### Quiz 1.5.1
Each of these sentences has an error. Find it and correct it.

1. If he would have asked me, I would have told him.

2. I would have bought some beer if I would have known David was coming.

3. Tom wishes he would have finished high school.

4. If the Knicks would have won, I would have made 50 bucks.

5. You wouldn't be so sick if you wouldn't have eaten like such a pig.

### 1.5.2 Using the past when the present perfect is better
Do these sound OK to you?

> *I didn't eat yet.*
> *He already spoke to her about the meeting tomorrow.*
> *Did you already see that movie?*

This is sort of a lost cause, but in the very best English, the present perfect would be better.

not the best English:  *I <u>didn't eat</u> yet.*
the best English:       *I <u>haven't eaten</u> yet.*

| not the best English: | *He already <u>spoke</u> to her about the meeting tomorrow.* |
| the best English: | *He <u>has</u> already <u>spoken</u> to her about the meeting tomorrow.* |

| not the best English: | *<u>Did</u> you already <u>see</u> that movie?* |
| the best English: | *<u>Have</u> you already <u>seen</u> that movie?* |

I'd advise you to be extra careful about this if there are any British members of the Grammar Police within earshot. This is a particular pet peeve of theirs regarding American English. (They act like they invented the language.)

## Quiz 1.5.2
Change these sentences so that they are the very best English.

1. I'm really hungry. I didn't eat all day.

2. Did you finish your homework yet?

3. We don't want to go there again. We already went there.

4. I told him to do it, but he still didn't do it.

5. She keeps saying she's going to quit smoking, but she still didn't.

### 1.5.3 Unnecessary use of the past perfect
Does this sound OK to you?

*Yesterday was a busy day. I had gone to the supermarket where I had bought a lot of things. Then, I had visited my friend in the hospital. Next, I had filled up my car with gas before I had returned home.*

If it does, then you don't understand what the past perfect is for. The past perfect is used when we talk about two events, both in the past, and we want to make it clear that one happened before the other. For example,

*I had lived here for three years before I met my neighbors.*
*Carlos didn't answer when I called because he had lost his phone.*

When people overuse the past perfect—using it when the simple past is all that's necessary—it's an example of *hypercorrection,* when people who have a sketchy understanding of grammar try to sound more formal.

In the paragraph above, there is no reason for the past perfect. This is just a series of unrelated past events, and which order they occurred in is of no importance because they have no relationship to each other.

*Yesterday was a busy day. I <u>went</u> to the supermarket where I <u>bought</u> a lot of things. Then, I <u>visited</u> my friend in the hospital. Next I <u>filled up</u> my car with gas before I <u>returned</u> home.*

### Quiz 1.5.3
Remove the unnecessary uses of the past perfect from this paragraph. (One of them is not unnecessary.)

Last week, my son had graduated from high school. We had attended his graduation and then had gone to a nice restaurant where we had had a nice dinner, and we had given him a new watch as a graduation present. After that, we had visited his grandparents. They had wanted to go out to dinner, but we told them that we had already had dinner.

## 1.5.4 Overdoing it with the present perfect

Do these sound OK to you?

> *I would have liked to have gone with you to the concert.*
> *Maria would have liked to have been there when we saw Bigfoot.*

If they do, you're getting carried away with the present perfect. One *have* is enough, but which one you get rid of depends on whether you're talking about how you feel now or how you felt at the time.

| | |
|---|---|
| one *have* too many: | *I would have liked to have gone with you to the concert.* |
| how you felt then: | *I would have liked to go with you to the concert.* |
| how you feel now: | *I would like to have gone with you to the concert.* |
| | |
| one *have* too many: | *Maria would have liked to have been there when we saw Bigfoot.* |
| how Maria felt then: | *Maria would have liked to be there when we saw Bigfoot.* |
| how Maria feels now: | *Maria would like to have been there when we saw Bigfoot.* |

## Quiz 1.5.4

Remove one use of the present perfect depending on whether you want to emphasize how you felt at the time or how you feel now.

*how you felt then:*

1. I'm sorry I missed Sarah. I would have liked to have seen her.

2. Why didn't you call me? I would have liked to have gone with you.

*how you feel now:*

3. That's funny! I would have liked to have been there when it happened.

4. I had no idea. I would have liked to have been informed of this in advance.

# 1.6 • Problems with Adjectives and Adverbs

## 1.6.1 Using adjectives when adverbs are correct

Do these sound OK to you?

> *My sister sings awful.*
> *I'm awful hungry.*
> *These cookies are real good.*
> *He's not taking this as serious as he should.*
> *My father drives so slow that it's dangerous.*
> *She did it perfect.*

WARNING!!! If they do, then keep reading because they're not OK, and this is an easy mistake for the Grammar Police to spot.

In each of the examples above, an adjective has been used when an adverb is needed. What's it all about? Adjectives describe nouns and adverbs describe verbs. Many adjectives can be turned into adverbs by adding *ly*.

    adjective describing noun:   *The answer is <u>correct</u>.*
    adverb describing verb:     *I answered the question <u>correctly</u>.*

The problem is that many people use adjectives when adverbs are correct. Don't be one of them! Here are some that are often used incorrectly, but there are more, so watch it!

### awful/awfully
Things are *awful,*

    *This coffee is <u>awful</u>.*

but people do things *awfully*. Sometimes people use *awful* when *awfully* is correct.

    wrong:   *My sister sings <u>awful</u>.*
    right:    *My sister sings <u>awfully</u>.*

In addition, *awfully,* like many other adverbs, can be used to modify adjectives and other adverbs, and for many people, that's the problem: They use *awful* when *awfully* is correct.

    wrong:   *I'm <u>awful</u> hungry.*
    right:    *I'm <u>awfully</u> hungry.*

    wrong:   *John works <u>awful</u> carelessly.*
    wrong:   *John works <u>awful</u> <u>careless</u>.*
    right:    *John works <u>awfully</u> <u>carelessly</u>.*

### beautiful/beautifully

    wrong:   *Nancy dances <u>beautiful</u>.*
    right:    *Nancy dances <u>beautifully</u>.*

### direct/directly

    wrong:   *I went <u>direct</u> to work.*
    right:    *I went <u>directly</u> to work.*

### loud/loudly

    wrong:   *The children were playing <u>loud</u>.*
    right:    *The children were playing <u>loudly</u>.*

### nice/nicely

    wrong:   *She sings <u>nice</u>.*
    right:    *She sings <u>nicely</u>.*

### perfect/perfectly

wrong:    *Carlos speaks Spanish <u>perfect</u>.*
right:    *Carlos speaks Spanish <u>perfectly</u>.*

### real/really

*Really*, like *awfully*, is often used to modify adjectives and other adverbs. Some people use *real* instead. Don't you be one of them.

wrong:    *These cookies are <u>real</u> good.*
right:    *These cookies are <u>really</u> good.*

wrong:    *Jennifer works <u>real</u> slowly.*
wrong:    *Jennifer works <u>real</u> <u>slow</u>.*
right:    *Jennifer works <u>really</u> <u>slowly</u>.*

### serious/seriously

wrong:    *He's not taking this as <u>serious</u> as he should.*
right:    *He's not taking this as <u>seriously</u> as he should.*

### slow/slowly

wrong:    *My father drives so <u>slow</u> that it's dangerous.*
right:    *My father drives so <u>slowly</u> that it's dangerous.*

### terrible/terribly

wrong:    *Kate plays tennis <u>terrible</u>.*
right:    *Kate plays tennis <u>terribly</u>.*

## Quiz 1.6.1

Some of these sentences have one or more errors. Find them and correct them.

1. Some of my students are awful dumb.

2. Doesn't Maria play the violin beautifully?

3. Michael drives terrible.

4. She made me terribly upset.

5. These cookies came out perfect.

6. Elaine dances awful.

7. That movie was awful. I hated it!

8. My neighbors were arguing real loud.

9. Thank you. That was real nice of you.

10. After that, I went directly to HR and told them the whole story.

11. Lisa is very sensitive, so treat her nice.

12. Francesca's cooking is awful.

13. Your plan is perfect.

14. Tom is real angry.

15. If you think that's a real diamond, you're real stupid.

16. Are you serious? That's the craziest thing I've ever heard of.

17. Hey! You'd better take me serious. I'm not joking.

18. This bus is so slow I think I could walk faster.

19. David is working so slow that I think he'll never finish this project.

20. We need to go direct to the airport. I don't have time to stop.

21. Will you please stop playing that music so loudly?

22. That was excellent! You did it just beautiful.

## 1.6.2 *less* vs. *fewer*
Do these sound OK to you?

> *Less people live in Chicago now than in 1950.*
> *February has less days than the other months.*

WARNING!!! OK, pay attention, because this extremely common mistake, confusing *less* and *fewer,* is one of the easiest mistakes for the Grammar Police to detect. Fortunately, it's also one of the easiest to fix.

Here's what it boils down to: In English we make a distinction between things that are countable and things that aren't (or aren't ordinarily) countable. Books, people, apples, pencils, etc. are countable. Food, water, salt, time and money are not. (Unless we discuss countable containers or quantities of uncountable things, but that's another matter.)

*Less* is used for things that are not countable.

> *My doctor told me to use <u>less salt</u>.*
> *I have <u>less energy</u> than when I was younger.*

*Fewer* is used for things that are countable.

> *<u>Fewer people</u> live in Chicago now than in 1950.*
> *February has <u>fewer days</u> than the other months.*

## Quiz 1.6.2
Some of these sentences have errors. Find them and correct them.

1. There are fewer students in the class I have now, so it takes less time for me to correct their homework.

2. Less than 1,000 people live in my town.

3. This system is better because it takes less time.

4. Fewer than 60 people live on Pitcairn Island.

5. I like shopping early in the morning because there are less people in the stores.

## 1.6.3 *very unique, extremely perfect, most complete,* etc.
Do these sound OK to you?

> *It was the most perfect day of my life.*
> *My new job is totally perfect.*
> *This guidebook is more complete than that one.*
> *Melanie has a very unique way of looking at things.*

WARNING!!! In casual speech, most members of the Grammar Police wouldn't be too troubled by these—we have worse crimes against the English language to worry about—but this is still something you should be aware of when you want to use the very best English.

Here's what it boils down to: *Unique* is like *pregnant* or *dead*—it's all or nothing. Someone or something either is or isn't; there's no in between. The same goes for *perfect* and *complete*. Adjectives like these (called *absolutes* by the Grammar Police) refer to maximum conditions, so logically, they can't be qualified. That means it doesn't make sense to speak of being *more, less, very, extremely, slightly, kind of* or *the most unique, complete* or *perfect*.

As I said, generally speaking, we members of the Grammar Police are lenient about this, but you should be aware of one thing that really gets on our nerves. *Very unique,* especially, is something that the Grammar Police are always on the alert for, so be extra careful about that.

So what should you do if you need to use the very best English? An easy way is to use *nearly.* Say *most nearly* or *more nearly,* and with words like *very, totally,* etc., simply eliminate them entirely or replace them with *nearly.* It will sound a bit stuffy, but you'll be speaking the very best English and be immune to criticism by the Grammar Police.

> *It was the most <u>nearly</u> perfect day of my life.*
> *My new job is perfect.*
> *This guidebook is more <u>nearly</u> complete than that one.*
> *Melanie has a unique way of looking at things.*
> *Melanie has a <u>nearly</u> unique way of looking at things.*

## Quiz 1.6.3
These sentences aren't totally horrible, but they can be improved.

1. It was an extremely perfect experience.

2. This is the most perfect diet I ever tried.

3. The police went back and did a more complete search of the suspect's house.

4. Venice is a very unique city.

5. Her engagement ring is totally unique. I've never seen another one like it.

### 1.6.4 *bad, badly, good* and *well*
Which word do you think is correct?

> *I feel (bad/badly) about the death of your father.*
> *I don't feel (good/well).*
> *My dog smells (bad/badly).*

First of all, unless the nerves in your finger tips are malfunctioning, *I feel badly,* no matter how common it is, is wrong. This is like fingernails on a chalkboard to the Grammar Police, so be careful.

> wrong:  *I feel <u>badly</u> about the death of your father.*
> right:  *I feel <u>bad</u> about the death of your father.*

Why *bad* and not *badly*? Because *bad* is an adjective, and adjectives describe nouns. That's why you *feel stupid, feel sick,* etc. *Badly* is an adverb, and adverbs describe verbs. That's why you *sing badly, dance badly, play tennis badly,* etc.

Now what about the second and third examples? Stumped? Hehe, I tricked you. In both examples, both words are correct. If you can feel *good,* you can feel the opposite, *bad.* And *well* is the opposite of *sick,* so if you *feel sick,* it means you don't *feel well.* What confuses people is the fact that *well* is both an adjective and an adverb.

> adjective:  *I don't feel <u>well</u>.*
> adverb:  *She speaks Japanese <u>well</u>.*
> adverb:  *Michael can't draw <u>well</u>.*

So, if your dog needs a bath, it smells *bad.* If it has a problem with its nose, it smells *badly.*

> adjective:  *Do you feel <u>bad</u> about hurting her feelings?*
> adverb:  *David plays basketball <u>badly</u>.*

Now that you've got that all figured out, explain this: *All's well that ends well.*

### Quiz 1.6.4
Each of these sentences has one or more errors. Find them and correct them.

1. I feel badly about hurting her feelings.

2. My wife speaks Spanish really good.

3. Mark feels badly because he did bad on the test.

4. Jim plays basketball really bad.

### 1.6.5 Placement of *only*
Do these sound OK to you?

*I only read three pages before I fell asleep.*
*I'm only going to explain this once.*

Well, even though these sound perfectly natural, even to me, a card-carrying member of the Grammar Police, they're not exactly correct. What it boils down to is that *only* logically belongs directly in front of what it is limiting. Here's what is exactly correct.

not exactly correct:    *I <u>only</u> read three pages before I fell asleep.*
exactly correct:       *I read <u>only</u> three pages before I fell asleep.*

not exactly correct:    *I'm <u>only</u> going to explain this one time.*
exactly correct:       *I'm going to explain this <u>only</u> one time.*

Putting *only* in front of the verb is so common that most members of the Grammar Police would likely give you a pass on this (and, egad!, many even do it themselves). But if you want to use the very best English, remember this because you live only once.

### Quiz 1.6.5
Each of these sentences isn't exactly correct. Make them exactly correct.

1. I only drank one cup of coffee.

2. She only wants two children.

3. Carlos is only going to the reception and not the wedding.

4. I'm sorry. I only said that because I was angry.

5. You're only allowed three sick days a year.

## 1.7 • Other Grammar Problems

### 1.7.1 Lack of parallel structure
Do these sound OK to you?

*I love playing tennis, riding my bike and to go swimming.*
*The manager told everyone that they should work harder, that they should get to work on time and to pay attention to detail.*

Does either of these seem awkward or unclear, even if you can't put your finger on exactly why? What's wrong with them is that they lack parallel structure. It boils down to this: Everything in a series or list (even if it's just two items) must be in the same form whether they're verbs, nouns, adjectives, prepositional phrases, etc. Let's rewrite the first example as follows.

*I love*
   *playing tennis*

*riding my bike*
*to go swimming*

Do you see how *to go swimming* is not in the same form as *playing tennis* and *riding my bike*? Here's how to fix it.

*I love*
parallel:        *playing tennis*
parallel:        *riding my bike and*
not parallel:  *to go swimming*
parallel:        *going swimming*

And here's the corrected sentence:

*I love playing tennis, riding my bike and going swimming.*

Let's fix the second example.

*The manager told everyone*
parallel:        *that they should work harder*
parallel:        *that they should get to work on time and*
not parallel:  *to pay attention to detail*
parallel:        *that they should pay attention to detail*

And here's the corrected sentence:

*The manager told everyone that they should get to work on time, that they should work harder and that they should pay attention to detail.*

Repeating *that they should* is optional. This would also be correct:

*The manager told everyone that they should work harder, get to work on time and pay attention to detail.*

Another area where parallel structure is important is in lists—lists like the bulleted or numbered lists you see in Microsoft Word or PowerPoint. All the elements must be in the same form—all adjectives, all adverbs, all nouns, all verbs (and if they're verbs, all in the same form).

*To maintain a healthy computer*
   *antivirus program*
   *don't open attachments to suspicious emails*
   *It's important to restart your computer regularly*
   *Laptops are prone to overheating—be careful about this.*

Let's take a scalpel to this list and see if we can save it. Starting every item in the list with a verb is the best solution:

*To maintain a healthy computer*
   <u>use</u> *an antivirus program*
   <u>don't open</u> *attachments to suspicious emails*
   <u>restart</u> *your computer regularly*
   <u>be</u> *careful not to let laptops overheat*

And as long as we're talking about PowerPoint lists, don't clutter them up with *and, or* or unnecessary punctuation. For example,

*To maintain a healthy computer,*
  *use an antivirus program,*
  *don't open attachments to suspicious emails,*
  *restart your computer regularly and*
  *be careful not to let laptops overheat.*

This looks amateurish.

## Quiz 1.7.1

Each of these sentences lacks parallel structure. Fix them.

1. Every evening, I make dinner, washing the dishes and do my homework.

2. My brother likes to swim, to play football and go fishing.

3. I hate waking up early and to work in the hot sun all day.

4. The boss likes me because I'm always on time, I do my work well and never complain.

5. To succeed in college, you must do the following: study hard, attending every class and taking notes is important.

## 1.7.2 *ten dollars worth of gas* or *ten dollars' worth of gas*?

When talking about quantities of time and money, it's correct to use a possessive noun. A singular possessive noun is made by adding *'s*. Most people know that, but many have forgotten that a plural possessive noun is made by adding *s'*. For example,

*The girl's name is Sarah.*
*The girls' names are Sarah and Lisa.*

And by the way, when a noun already has plural built into it, like *people, children, feet* and *men,* then possession is shown with *'s*.

*The children's teacher is very strict.*
*I bought some new shirts at a men's clothing store.*

Here are more examples of how to use possessive nouns with quantities of time and money.

*I lost five years' of work on my book when my computer crashed.*
*She gave her boss two weeks' notice.*
*In an hour's time, the new law will take effect.*
*My son charged a hundred dollars' worth of beer on my credit card.*
*You always get your money's worth at this store.*

## Quiz 1.7.2

Each of these sentences has an error. Find it and correct it.

1. My landlord requires a months notice before ending the rental agreement.

2. I bought twenty dollars worth of gas.

3. In ten days time I'll be in Cancun.

4. He'll be out of jail in three years time.

5. My stupid husband lost two months salary in Las Vegas.

### 1.7.3 *I don't got*
Do these sound OK to you?

> *I don't got any money.*
> *We don't got to work tomorrow.*

WARNING!!! I hope not. If they do, read on. These are mutants—grotesque combinations of two perfectly correct grammatical structures. In the case of the first example,

> *I don't have any money. + I haven't got any money.*

and the second example.

> *We don't have to work tomorrow. + We haven't got to work tomorrow.*

What it boils down to is this: In English, instead of *have* and *have to,* we can say *have got* and *have got to.* All of them are correct. Just don't mix them. And in case you're dying to know, *have got* and *have got to* are what we members of the Grammar Police call *idioms*—things that all native speakers use and understand that don't actually make sense grammarwise. Other examples are *so long* (Why should *so long* mean *good bye?*), *by and large, make do, at all* and *how come* (How come *how come* means *why?*). In the case of *have got* and *have got to, got* means absolutely nothing. Go figure.

## Quiz 1.7.3
Each of these sentences has an error. Find it and correct it. Try to use both of the structures discussed in the lesson.

1. Do you got to work on Saturday?

2. I don't got a car.

3. They don't got to hand in their homework till next week.

4. What do we got to do tomorrow?

5. She don't got a penny to her name.

### 1.7.4 *may have* or *might have?*
Do these sound OK to you?

> a. *I was attacked by a mountain lion last week. I may have been killed.*
> b. *Carlos should have been here 10 minutes ago. He might have stopped for gas.*
> c. *I saw Sarah yesterday. She told me that she was in a bad accident last month and may have died.*

d. *David went scuba diving yesterday, and now he's missing. He may have been eaten by a shark.*

e. *It's a good thing I had my GPS. Otherwise I may have gotten lost.*

f. *Your parachute didn't open? Wow, you might have been killed.*

g. *The plane is one hour late. It may have crashed.*

h. *I'll ask Jim if he wants to see* Zombies Ate My Brain *with us, but I think he might have seen it already.*

i. *Sam didn't come to my party last night. I think he may have forgotten about it.*

Here's a hint: Six are OK; three are wrong.

Give up? Here's what it boils down to: When we are talking about something unknown, both *may have* and *might have* are OK, but when we are talking about something that is known, only *might have* is correct. That means examples *a, c* and *e* are wrong. In each case we are talking about something that could have happened that we know did not happen. I wasn't killed by the mountain lion, Sarah didn't die and I didn't get lost. So remember,

| unknown: | either *may have* or *might have* |
|---|---|
| known: | only *might have* |

| wrong: | *I was attacked by a mountain lion last week. I <u>may</u> have been killed.* |
|---|---|
| right: | *I was attacked by a mountain lion last week. I <u>might</u> have been killed.* |

| wrong: | *I saw Sarah yesterday. She told me that she was in a bad accident last month and <u>may</u> have died.* |
|---|---|
| right: | *I saw Sarah yesterday. She told me that she was in a bad accident last month and <u>might</u> have died.* |

| wrong: | *It's a good thing I had my GPS. Otherwise I <u>may</u> have gotten lost.* |
|---|---|
| right: | *It's a good thing I had my GPS. Otherwise I <u>might</u> have gotten lost.* |

## Quiz 1.7.4
Some of these sentences have errors. Find them and correct them.

1. Phew, that meteor missed me by just a few inches. If it had hit me, I may have been killed.

2. I'm worried. I think my boss may have discovered that I embezzled some money.

3. Jim told me he may have gotten lost on the way here if it weren't for his GPS.

4. The policeman told me he may have been killed if he hadn't been wearing a bulletproof vest.

5. I wonder where Sofia is. I think she may have forgotten that I invited her for dinner tonight.

## 1.7.5 *where's it at?* or *where is it?*
This is an easy one.

not good:  *Where's <u>it at</u>?*

better:     *Where is it?*

The same is true of statements.

not good:   *I don't know where it's at.*
better:     *I don't know where it is.*

### 1.7.6 *the reason is because*
Another easy one. When you say *reason*, you don't need to say *because*.

not good:   *The reason is because*
better:     *The reason is*
better:     *The reason is that*

### 1.7.7 *try and*
Try to get this right if you want to use the very best English.

not good:   *try and*
better:     *try to*

### 1.7.8 *be sure and*
Be sure to get this right if you want to use the very best English.

not good:   *be sure and*
better:     *be sure to*

### Quiz 1.7.5-1.7.8
Each of these sentences is not good. Try to make them better.

1. Where's my cell phone at?

2. I have no idea where it's at.

3. I'm going to try and get my boss to give me Friday off.

4. My father told me to be sure and lock the door when I leave.

5. Why do I want to quit my job? The reason is because the pay is so low.

### 1.7.9 *like* or *as*?
Before a clause, which means a group of words with a subject and a verb, some snooty members of the Grammar Police prefer *as* rather than *like*. More liberal-minded members of the Grammar Police feel that *like* is acceptable. I tend to agree, but if you want to sound extra formal and snooty, use *as*.

OK:                             *You didn't do it like I told you to do it.*
extra formal and snooty:        *You didn't do it as I told you to do it.*

### 1.7.10 *like* or *such as*?
Some snooty members of the Grammar Police also feel that *such as* is better than *like,* but either is acceptable. There's nothing wrong with *like,* but use *such as* if you want to sound extra formal and snooty.

| OK: | *The store sells things <u>like</u> hammers, saws, wrenches and screw drivers.* |
| extra formal and snooty: | *The store sells things <u>such as</u> hammers, saws, wrenches and screw drivers.* |

## Quiz 1.7.9-1.7.10

There's nothing wrong with these sentences, but they are not extra formal and snooty. Try to make them extra formal and snooty.

1. The construction guys didn't build the deck like I asked them to.

2. My father would never eat food like clams or oysters.

3. On a low carb diet you need to avoid foods like bread, rice and pasta.

4. He screwed it up just like I knew he would.

5. I would never want to live in a hot, humid city like Houston or New Orleans.

## 1.7.11 *used to/didn't use to*

Be sure you use the right form.

wrong:   *I <u>use to</u> live France.*
right:     *I <u>used to</u> live France.*

wrong:   *I didn't <u>used to</u> live in Germany.*
right:     *I didn't <u>use to</u> live in Germany.*

wrong:   *Did you <u>used to</u> smoke?*
right:     *Did you <u>use to</u> smoke?*

## Quiz 1.7.11

Each of these sentences has an error. Find it and correct it.

1. Where did you used to work?

2. Didn't you used to be a lot thinner?

3. My father use to have truck.

4. Did he used to live in Alaska?

5. I always use to think he was an idiot, and I was right.

## 1.7.12 Verbs must be agreeable

Which word do you think is correct?

a. *The only common link between the two murders (was/were) the gun.*
b. *My car—the engine, the body and the tires—(is/are) in terrible condition.*
c. *The house, along with all the furnishings and appliances, (was/were) sold for $425,000.*
d. *She's one of the students who always (get/gets) good grades.*

e. *Not one of the applicants (has/have) the right qualifications.*
f. *One of the towns that (is/are) being considered for the new plant is Springfield.*
g. *One of the things the investigators looked at (was/were) the speed of the aircraft.*

We English teachers love to talk about *subject-verb agreement.* It's what gets us out of bed in the morning. What it boils down to is that the verb in a sentence must be in the form that is correct for the subject. It's easy enough to do in a short sentence where the verb directly follows the subject.

*He lives in Canada.* (*Lives* is obviously correct, not *live.*)
*They are crazy.* (No danger of using *am* or *is.*)

But sometimes people get confused when the subject and verb are separated by extra information, and they end up using the wrong verb form. The key to avoiding this is to identify the subject, ignore the extra information and make sure the verb is correct for that subject.

Let's try that with examples *a, b* and *c.* We'll isolate the subject and get rid of the extra information. Then the correct verb form will be clear.

a. *The only common link was*
b. *My car is*
c. *The house was*

But did you have any trouble with *d, e, f* and *g? One* can be tricky because it can go both ways. It depends on who or what the subject is—one member of a group or the entire group. It it's one member of the group, we need a singular verb. If it's the entire group, we need a plural verb. Let's identify the subjects in *d, e, f* and *g.*

d. *She's one of the students who always (get/gets) good grades.*
e. *Not one of the applicants (has/have) the right qualifications.*
f. *One of the towns that (is/are) being considered for the new plant is Springfield.*
g. *One of the things the investigators looked at (was/were) the speed of the aircraft.*

And here are the verb forms that agree with those subjects:

d. *the students get*
e. *one has*
f. *the towns are*
g. *one was*

## Quiz 1.7.12
Each of these sentences has an error. Find it and correct it.

1. Not a single student in any of the math classes have a chance of passing the test.

2. Sean is one of my cousins who lives in France.

3. One of the people that was at the party was kind of weird.

4. One of the things that bothers me about him is how much he drinks

5. Dr. Smith is one of the few people who understands quantum physics.

### 1.7.13 *and stuff*
Do these sound OK to you?

> *Let's go to the mall and stuff.*
> *Did you finish all your work and stuff?*
> *On Saturday we always clean the house and stuff before we go grocery shopping.*

People make all kinds of mistakes and stuff with English, and it can make a bad impression and stuff on other people.

It hurt just writing that. If you're in the habit of saying, *and stuff,* stop right now! (Unless you want to sound like a 15-year-old.) People say this when they're too lazy or clueless to come up with a word that actually describes what they're thinking. It sounds dreadful.

But there's nothing wrong with using *stuff* as a word for miscellaneous items (i.e. nouns), as long as you're speaking informally. Otherwise, use *things* or *items.* (And remember, always be specific about stuff.)

### 1.7.14 *I'm like*
As a member of the Grammar Police, when I hear people make grammar mistakes, I'm like OMG!

Unless you want to sound like a 15-year-old, I strongly advise you not to say *I'm like.* Instead, talk about how you felt, what you said or what you wanted to say.

### Quiz 1.7.13-1.7.14
Each of these sentences would make you sound like a 15-year-old. Rewrite them in order to avoid that.

1. The doctor prescribed antibiotics and stuff.

2. When he told me he wanted to quit his job and join the circus, I'm like no way!

## 1.8 • Grammar Myths
It's ironic that the only grammar rules many people remember aren't rules at all—they're myths. Here are some that you can stop believing.

### 1.8.1 The passive voice should be avoided like the plague (along with clichés)
First of all, if you're not sure what I mean by *the passive voice* (often called simply *the passive*), here are some examples, along with the alternative to the passive voice, called *the active voice.*

active:   *Somebody <u>stole</u> my car.*
passive:  *My car <u>was</u> <u>stolen</u> by somebody.*

active:   *People <u>speak</u> Spanish in Peru.*
passive:  *Spanish <u>is</u> <u>spoken</u> in Peru by people.*

active:   *A mechanic <u>is</u> <u>fixing</u> my car.*

passive: *My car is being fixed by a mechanic.*

active: *A delivery guy will deliver the package tomorrow.*
passive: *The package will be delivered tomorrow by a delivery guy.*

For reasons that are a mystery to me, some misguided members of the Grammar Police maintain that the passive voice should be avoided at all costs. This is nonsense. The passive serves a purpose, and what that purpose is I'll explain right now. Look at the active examples above. Do they seem kind of dumb? Isn't the information at the beginning of the sentence—*Somebody, People* (as opposed to llamas?), *A mechanic, A delivery guy*—kind of obvious? Is it really necessary to provide this information? Now you see one of the reasons we use the passive. When the person doing the action of the verb is unknown, unimportant or obvious, the passive allows us to avoid mentioning that person at all. A *by*-phrase is always possible, as we see in the examples above, but not always necessary. Don't these seem better?

*My car was stolen.*
*Spanish is spoken in Peru.*
*My car is being fixed.*
*The package will be delivered tomorrow.*

But sometimes, even though we want to emphasize the action of the verb and who or what received that action, the doer of the verb is worth mentioning, and then we can.

*My car was stolen by my useless stepson.*
*Spanish is spoken in Peru by 85% of the population.*
*My car is being fixed by Tony at Joe's Garage.*
*The package will be delivered tomorrow by DHL.*

There is no particular reason why the passive should be avoided by you although, obviously, it should not be overdone by you because if it is used too much by you, your writing and speaking can be made to sound bloated, pompous and ridiculous.

## 1.8.2 Never begin a sentence with a conjunction

There are different kinds of conjunctions. In this case, it's the coordinating conjunctions *and, but, for, nor, or, so,* and *yet* that we're talking about (and usually *and, but* and *or*). Some people who don't know what they are talking about maintain that beginning a sentence with one of these conjunctions is a crime against the English language. And this is nonsense. Did you see what I just did? I began a sentence with a conjunction in order to make a shift in tone a little more dramatic than if I had said *…against the English language, and this is nonsense.*

Compare these pairs of sentences and decide which of the two has a little more drama, a little more punch.

*Nicholas thought he had gotten away with murder, but he was wrong.*
*Nicholas thought he had gotten away with murder. But he was wrong.*

*We could reason with him to make him understand, or we could kill him.*
*We could reason with him to make him understand. Or we could kill him.*

*He lied to his wife that the woman she had seen him with was his sister, and she knew it was a lie.*
*He lied to his wife that the woman she had seen him with was his sister. And she knew it was a lie.*

I'm sure you agree that in every case, the second sentence has more impact. So feel free to begin sentences with conjunctions on occasion. But don't overdo it.

### 1.8.3 Never end a sentence with a preposition

This nonsense dates from long ago when early members of the Grammar Police had the silly notion that English should follow the rules of Latin grammar. It's absolute baloney. Feel free to end a sentence with a preposition whenever you want to.

### 1.8.4 Never split an infinitive

An infinitive is the form of the verb that often follows *to*, for example,

*I want to eat.*
*You need to be here at 8:00.*

A myth believed by many is that nothing should ever come between *to* and the verb. They would say that the following sentences are wrong. (They are not wrong.)

*The company decided to gradually raise the price by 10%.*
*You need to finally get it through your head that she's not coming back.*

The notion that you should never split an infinitive is nonsense—another pointless attempt from long ago to force English to conform to the rules of Latin grammar. Infinitives in Latin are single words; they cannot be split. In English they can be. Feel free to boldly split infinitives whenever you please.

### 1.8.5 *None* should always be singular

Many misguided members of the Grammar Police believe that *none* should always be singular. They would have you say, for example,

*None of the apples is ripe.*
*None of the people in the car was wearing a seatbelt.*

If those examples sound a bit awkward, it's because they are awkward. There is no reason whatever to use the singular verb. Both are perfectly correct, and not awkward, with plural verbs.

*None of the apples are ripe.*
*None of the people in the car were wearing a seatbelt.*

### Quiz 1.8.1-1.8.5

These sentences may contain errors. If you find any, correct them.

1. The policeman asked me where I had come from.

2. My boss said, "It has been noticed that you have been returning from lunch drunk."

3. And then she said, "You're fired."

4. She told me to immediately go to my office, collect my things and leave the premises.

5. I've sent my résumé to several companies, but none of them are interested.

## 2.1 • Frequently Messed Up Words

### 2.1.1 *a whole nother*

WARNING!!! No such word as *nother*. Be careful about this. The Grammar Police think it's kind of dumb.

| | |
|---|---|
| wrong and kind of dumb: | *That's a whole nother thing.* |
| right: | *That's another thing.* |
| right: | *That's a whole new thing.* |
| right: | *That's a whole other thing.* |
| right: | *That's a completely different thing.* |

### 2.1.2 *abolition* or *abolishment*?

*Abolishment* isn't incorrect, but many people think it is, and since the Grammar Police prefer *abolition,* it's better to use that.

| | |
|---|---|
| OK: | *We learned about the <u>abolishment</u> of slavery in school today.* |
| better: | *We learned about the <u>abolition</u> of slavery in school today.* |

### 2.1.3 *burst* or *bust*?

*Bust* is correct only if you're talking about getting busted by the police. Otherwise, use *burst* or *break.*

| | |
|---|---|
| wrong: | *The balloon <u>busted</u>.* |
| right: | *The balloon <u>burst</u>.* |
| wrong: | *I <u>busted</u> a window.* |
| right: | *I <u>broke</u> a window.* |
| wrong: | *The window is <u>busted</u>.* |
| right: | *The window is <u>broken</u>.* |

### 2.1.4 *compare to* or *compare with*?

They're both correct but not the same.

Use *compare to* when talking about the resemblance of one thing to something in a different class or category. The focus is on similarities.

*He <u>compared</u> the steaks <u>to</u> pieces of shoe leather.*

Use *compare with* when talking about two things in the same class or category. The focus is on the differences.

*<u>Compared</u> <u>with</u> my house, her house is bigger but has a smaller yard.*

In most cases, *compare with* is what you want, so if you're not sure, stick with that.

### 2.1.5 *comprises* or *is comprised of*?

Which of these sound OK to you?

> a. *The USA comprises 50 states.*
> b. *The USA is comprised of 50 states.*

It might surprise you, but *a* is preferred by the Grammar Police. They frown upon *is comprised of.*

> frowned upon by the Grammar Police:   *A baseball team <u>is comprised of</u> nine players.*
> preferred by the Grammar Police:       *A baseball team <u>comprises</u> nine players.*

### 2.1.6 *coronated* or *crowned*?

Kings and queens are not *coronated.* They are *crowned* at their *coronation.*

> wrong:   *Queen Elizabeth was <u>coronated</u> in 1953.*
> right:     *Queen Elizabeth was <u>crowned</u> in 1953.*

### 2.1.7 *decimate*

Last time you fought in a battle, was your side *decimated*? That's good because it means 90% of you lived to fight another day. *Decimate* does not mean that you or your team or your side, etc. was destroyed or damaged in some overwhelming way, as many people believe. The word comes from the Roman practice of executing every tenth man in a rebellious army. (They didn't mess around.) So think twice before you use this word. Some people, especially the Grammar Police or any Roman soldiers you may know, will notice that you've used the word incorrectly.

### 2.1.8 *different from* or *different than*?

When you're talking about nouns, *different from* is right and *different than* is not.

> wrong:   *My plan is <u>different than</u> her plan.*
> right:     *My plan is <u>different from</u> her plan.*

But *different than* isn't always wrong. It is correct with a clause, which just means a group of words with a subject and a verb.

> correct:        *Jim's new wife was <u>different than</u> I thought she would be.*
> also correct:  *Jim's new wife was <u>different from how</u> I thought she would be.*

> correct:        *The hotel was <u>different than</u> I expected it to be.*
> also correct:  *The hotel was <u>different from what</u> I expected it to be.*

And just to complicate things, our British friends insist on saying *different to* rather than *different from.*

### 2.1.9 *disrespect* used as a verb

*Disrespect* has long been used as a noun, but in recent years it has become increasingly common to use it as a verb. This use has a long history, and isn't wrong, but because its use as a verb fell out of favor for a long time and has only recently been revived, it sounds wrong to many members of the Grammar Police. If you want to keep them from looking at you funny, avoid using *disrespect* as a verb.

frowned upon by the Grammar Police:     *David disrespected me.*

not frowned upon by the Grammar Police:     *David treated me with disrespect.*

## 2.1.10 *foot* or *feet*?

The plural of the measurement *foot* is *feet,* not *foot.*

wrong:  *I bought ten foot of rope.*
right:  *I bought ten feet of rope.*

Don't be confused by sentences like *I bought a ten-foot rope.* In this case, *ten* and *foot* are joined together to make a compound adjective (discussed in 3.3.2). *Foot* and *feet* in the examples above are nouns.

## 2.1.11 *hopefully*

WARNING!!! This a particular pet peeve of many members of the Grammar Police, so watch out. Many believe that using *hopefully* like this:

*Hopefully, the weather will be nice when we have our annual company picnic.*

is not just wrong but the grammatical crime of the century. They believe people should instead say

*It is to be hoped that the weather will be nice when we have our annual company picnic.*

That sounds as stuffy to me as it does to you, so I don't recommend it. Instead, when you want your English to be immune to criticism by the Grammar Police, just avoid *hopefully* entirely. And just between you and me, some members of the Grammar Police don't see anything wrong with *hopefully.* I don't.

## 2.1.12 *hung* or *hanged*?

They're both correct, but it depends on who or what you're hanging. Pictures are *hung.* Criminals are *hanged.*

*I hung a painting in my living room.*
*The murderer was hanged at dawn.*

## 2.1.13 *ice tea* or *iced tea*?, *old fashion* or *old fashioned*?, *whip cream* or *whipped cream*?

In each case, the *ed* version is correct. This may change someday—*ice cream* is accepted—but for the others, stick to the *ed* version. (See 3.3.2 for an explanation of when a hyphen is required with *old fashioned.*)

wrong:  *My wife ordered ice tea, our son ordered pumpkin pie with whip cream, and I drank an old fashion.*
right:  *My wife ordered iced tea, our son ordered pumpkin pie with whipped cream, and I drank an old fashioned.*

## 2.1.14 *between* or *in between*?

When *between* is used as a preposition, there's no need for *in*, so *in between, in-between* or (yikes!) *inbetween* are just plain wrong.

wrong:   *I had to sit <u>in between</u> two huge guys on a 14-hour-flight.*
right:   *I had to sit <u>between</u> two huge guys on a 14-hour-flight.*

### 2.1.15 *in to* or *into*?

Use *in to* when *to* is followed by a verb in the infinitive form (for example, *to eat, to go*),

*I dropped <u>in to see</u> if you needed any help.*
*The manager stepped <u>in to give</u> the workers a hand.*

but use *into* when you're talking about moving to or entering a place.

*I walked <u>into the room</u>.*
*Nicholas fell <u>into a vat</u> of boiling oil.*

If you're not sure, remember this: If the sentence makes sense with *in order to,* then *in to* is what you need. If the sentence answers the question *where?*, then *into* is what you need.

### 2.1.16 *irregardless*

WARNING!!! Regardless of what you hear many people say, there is no such word as *irregardless*. Be careful about this one. The Grammar Police hate it.

wrong:   *She is always cheerful <u>irregardless</u> of her problems.*
right:   *She is always cheerful <u>regardless</u> of her problems.*

### 2.1.17 *literally*

WARNING!!! There are few ways more certain than this to make the Grammar Police think you're a dumbbell (which you may be). It's a very common mistake. I must hear it literally a million times a day.

Do I really hear it a million times a day? No, of course I don't. I was exaggerating, and saying I *literally* hear it a million times a day makes no sense at all and sounds really dumb to the Grammar Police because *literally* means *really, truly, actually.* It means you are NOT exaggerating. So be careful about this!

### 2.1.18 *memento* or *momento*?

Easy. There's no such word as *momento* in the English language, so using it is just plain wrong. Only *memento* is correct. Just remember that a <u>memento</u> is something that brings back <u>memories,</u> something that helps you <u>remember.</u>

wrong:   *I have many <u>momentos</u> from my travels.*
right:   *I have many <u>mementos</u> from my travels.*

### 2.1.19 *more important* or *more importantly*?

Which word do you think is correct?

*The car was only slightly damaged and, more (important/importantly), no one was hurt or killed.*

Members of the Grammar Police have been squabbling about this one for years. Many believe that *more importantly* is an abomination and that only *more im-*

*portant* is correct. Others point out that *more importantly* can properly modify an entire sentence the same way, for example, that *fortunately* or *thankfully* can. I agree that there is nothing wrong with *more importantly,* but that's not the point. The point is that because, right or wrong, many members of the Grammar Police don't approve of *more importantly,* if you want to stay on their good side, you should avoid it and say *more important.* (All of this applies to *most important* and *most importantly* as well.)

## 2.1.20 *oblivious of* or *oblivious to*?

*Oblivious to* is more common than *oblivious of.* Both are correct.

OK:  *Many people are <u>oblivious of</u> correct grammar, spelling, punctuation and pronunciation.*

OK:  *Many people are <u>oblivious to</u> correct grammar, spelling, punctuation and pronunciation.*

## 2.1.21 *on to* or *onto*?

*Onto* is about movement. It could be replaced with *upon, on top of* or simply *on.*

*The pigeon droppings fell <u>onto</u> my head.*
= *The pigeon droppings fell <u>upon</u> my head.*
= *The pigeon droppings fell <u>on top of</u> my head.*
= *The pigeon droppings fell <u>on</u> my head.*

*My cat jumped <u>onto</u> the table.*
= *My cat jumped <u>upon</u> the table.*
= *My cat jumped <u>on top of</u> the table.*
= *My cat jumped <u>on</u> the table.*

If *upon, on top of* or *on* don't work, use *on to.*

*I held <u>on to</u> my daughter's hand as we crossed the street.*
*She moved <u>on to</u> the next topic.*

In this case, the verbs are *prepositional verbs,* verbs which always require a preposition, like *look at* or *listen to* (often called, not entirely correctly, *phrasal verbs*). In the last two examples, you could ask

question:  *What did you do?*
answer:  *I <u>held on</u>.*

or

question:  *What did she do?*
answer:  *She <u>moved on</u>.*

But try that with the examples at the top, and you'll see that the answers don't make sense.

question:  *What did the pigeon droppings do?*
answer that doesn't make sense:  *They fell <u>onto</u>.*

question: *What did your cat do?*
answer that doesn't make sense: *He jumped <u>onto</u>.*

## 2.1.22 *pair* or *pairs*?

Easy. The plural of *pair* is *pairs*. Using *pair* as the plural is very common but just plain wrong.

wrong: *I bought two <u>pair</u> of pants and three <u>pair</u> of socks.*
right: *I bought two <u>pairs</u> of pants and three <u>pairs</u> of socks.*

## 2.1.23 *per say* or *per se*?

Easy. No such word as *per say.*

wrong: *She wasn't so much concerned with her son's speeding tickets <u>per say</u> but what they indicate about his sense of responsibility.*
right: *She wasn't so much concerned with her son's speeding tickets <u>per se</u> but what they indicate about his sense of responsibility.*

## 2.1.24 *percentage* or *percent*?

This is kind of a lost cause, but we members of the Grammar Police still make a distinction between *percent* and *percentage,* and we prefer that you get it right. It's not difficult. Here's what it boils down to:

Use *percent* when discussing a specific amount. You can use the word, *percent,* or the symbol, *%,* which would be spoken as *percent.*

*In my opinion, at least <u>90%</u> of the members of the Grammar Police need to get a life. Only <u>30 percent</u> of the students passed the test.*

By the way, when a number is used with the word *percent,* as in the second example, always use a numeral (rather than the word), even with small numbers.

Otherwise, use *percentage.*

*What <u>percentage</u> of Canadians speak French? Only a small <u>percentage</u> of people who contract this disease survive.*

## 2.1.25 *preventive* or *preventative*?

Both are correct, but since many members of the Grammar Police prefer *preventive,* you're better off sticking with that.

OK: *<u>Preventative</u> medicine is the best medicine.*
preferred by the Grammar Police: *<u>Preventive</u> medicine is the best medicine.*

## 2.1.26 Extra *s*-itis

A disease affecting some words is the growth of an incorrect and totally unnecessary *s* at the end of the word. If your vocabulary is infected with extra *s*-itis, you need to get out the scalpel.

wrong: *alls*
right: *all*

| wrong: | *anyways* |
|--------|-----------|
| right: | *anyway* |

| wrong: | *anywheres* |
|--------|-------------|
| right: | *anywhere* |

| wrong: | *sos* |
|--------|-------|
| right: | *so* |

| wrong: | *ways* |
|--------|--------|
| right: | *way* |

But some words that have an *s* version are correct either way: *toward, towards, backward, backwards, forward, forwards, upward, upwards, downward, downwards.* These are all correct.

## Quiz 2.1.1-2.1.26

Each of these sentences has an error or can be improved. Either correct them or improve them.

1. If you're traveling in Switzerland, be sure to take alot of money.

2. Oh, I see. That's a whole nother thing.

3. In school today we studied the abolishment of slavery.

4. Sorry to bust your balloon, Lisa, but he's lying to you.

5. My mother didn't think it was funny when I compared her corned beef hash with dog food.

6. I compared my plan to his, and mine is better in every way.

7. New York City is comprised of five boroughs.

8. The new king will be coronated next week.

9. The terrorist cell was decimated. There wasn't a single survivor.

10. How is American English different than British English?

11. I need to buy 20 foot of rope.

12. Captain Kidd was hung in 1701.

13. My father had a lot of old fashion ideas.

14. The shoe store is in between the book store and the supermarket.

15. The cannibals dropped the missionary in to a cauldron of boiling water.

16. When my mother didn't answer the door, I had to break into see if she was OK.

17. I'm going to buy a Ferrari irregardless of what my wife says.

18. I've told you literally a billion times. The answer is no.

19. These momentos bring back a lot of memories.

20. Carlos rescued a man who fell on to the subway tracks.

21. I turned the TV onto watch the game.

22. My wife bought two pair of shoes and three pair of pants.

23. I wonder what percent of people are left-handed.

24. It's quite a ways from here to there.

25. Anyways, alls I called about was to ask you if you want to go anywheres tomorrow, sos if you do, let me know.

## 2.2 • Frequently Messed Up Verb Forms

WARNING!!! Verbs, words like *come, go, eat* and *sleep,* have forms that you need to get right if you want to stay out of trouble with the Grammar Police. The present form has two variations, one with *s* and one without (*I live in Chicago, He lives in Chicago*). There's also the past form and the past participle, the form we use with *perfect tenses* (*I have eaten, He had died*), the *passive voice* (*My car was stolen*) and sometimes as adjectives (*I have a broken arm*). Some people make mistakes with these forms, and believe me, this is something the Grammar Police notice.

Some verbs are *regular.* That means the past form and the past participle are the same—both have *ed* stuck on the end. For example, the past form and past participle of *work* are both *worked.*

But other verbs, called *irregular verbs,* are all over the map. They don't have *ed,* and the past form and past participle are sometimes different and sometimes not. This is where people often get into trouble.

In addition, all verbs have what's called the *infinitive* form. It's the form of the verb we would use after *to.* With one major exception, it's always the same as the present form except when the present form has an *s* stuck on the end. The one important exception is *be. Be* is the infinitive (*I'm going to be late*) but the present forms are *am, is* and *are.*

Here is a rundown of some verbs that many people have trouble with, and because many past participles are used as adjectives, some of the adjective forms that people have trouble with too. Remember, only these forms are correct.

### 2.2.1 *blow/blew/blown*

| | |
|---|---|
| present: | Don't <u>blow</u> up the chemistry lab. |
| past: | He <u>blew</u> out the candle. (not *blowed*!) |
| past participle: | The wind has <u>blown</u> all day. (not *blowed*!) |

### 2.2.2 *break/broke/broken*

present:          *I never <u>break</u> the law.*
past:              *He <u>broke</u> a glass.*
past participle: *Maria has <u>broken</u> her arm.* (not *broke!*)
adjective:       *The window is <u>broken</u>.* (not *broke!*)

### 2.2.3 *come/came/come*

present:          *<u>Come</u> here now.*
past:              *He <u>came</u> to class late.* (not *come!*)
past participle: *He has <u>come</u> to class late every day this week.* (not *came!*)

### 2.2.4 *do/did/done*

present:          *I always <u>do</u> the dishes after dinner.*
past:              *Lisa <u>did</u> her homework in the library.* (not *done!*)
past participle: *I haven't <u>done</u> anything wrong.* (not *did!*)

### 2.2.5 *dive/dived/dived*

*Dived* or *dove*? Who hasn't agonized over this? Well agonize no more. *Dived* is preferred by the Grammar Police.

present:          *Let's <u>dive</u> into this shallow water.*
past:              *I <u>dived</u> into the shallow water.* (not *dove!*)
past participle: *If I hadn't <u>dived</u> into the shallow water, I wouldn't be in this wheel chair now.* (not *dove!*)

### 2.2.6 *drag/dragged/dragged*

present:          *I need to <u>drag</u> this dead guy outside.*
past:              *I <u>dragged</u> another dead guy outside yesterday.* (not *drug!*)
past participle: *I have <u>dragged</u> several dead guys outside recently.* (not *drug!*)

### 2.2.7 *drink/drank/drunk*

present:          *This coffee is too hot to <u>drink</u>.*
past:              *My ex <u>drank</u> like a fish.*
past participle: *Someone has <u>drunk</u> all my beer.* (not *drank!*)

### 2.2.8 *drive/drove/driven*

present:          *I <u>drive</u> to work every day.*
past:              *I <u>drove</u> to work yesterday.*
past participle: *I have <u>driven</u> to work every day for years.* (not *drove!*)

### 2.2.9 *go/went/gone*

WARNING!!! *I should have went,* or variations of that, is a very common mistake, and it sounds horrible to the Grammar Police, so if you're saying this, stop right now!

| present: | *I go there every Saturday.* |
| past: | *I went there last Saturday.* (not *goed!*) |
| past participle: | *I have gone there many times.* (not *went!*) |

## 2.2.10 *lie/lay/lain* (as in *lie down*, not *lie* as in *not tell the truth*)

WARNING!!! Pay attention to *lie* and to *lay*, which follows. This is one of the most common mistakes in this book, and it's also one of the biggest pet peeves of the Grammar Police. With their extra sensitive ears, they can detect a mistake with *lie* and *lay* a mile away. But the good news is that it's not that difficult to get it right and that getting it right is a great way to impress the Grammar Police as well as your friends and neighbors, especially if they happen to be English teachers.

What it boils down to is that *lie* is something you do yourself or something that something does itself, and lay is something you do to something else or in the case of a baby, somebody else.

| wrong: | *I like to lay on the beach.* |
| right: | *I like to lie on the beach.* |

| wrong: | *Why are your clothes laying on the floor?* |
| right: | *Why are your clothes lying on the floor?* |

| wrong: | *I laid out in the sun yesterday.* |
| right: | *I lay out in the sun yesterday.* |

| wrong: | *I've laid here all day with a headache.* |
| right: | *I've lain here all day with a headache.* |

| present: | *All my son does is lie on the sofa and watch TV.* |
| past: | *He lay on the sofa all day yesterday.* (not *laid!*) |
| past participle: | *He has lain on the sofa for hours doing nothing.* (yep, *lain*, not *laid!*) |

## 2.2.11 *lay/laid/laid* (See also *lie* above.)

| present: | *I'll lay the baby in his crib.* |
| past: | *She laid her book down and turned off the light.* |
| past participle: | *I've laid the papers on the desk.* |

## 2.2.12 *lead/led/led*

| present: | *Wherever you lead, I will follow.* |
| past: | *The sergeant led the attack on the enemy position.* (not *lead!*) |
| past participle: | *The new law hasn't led to a reduction in the crime rate.* (not *lead!*) |

## 2.2.13 *ride/rode/ridden*

| present: | *He rides his bike every day.* |
| past: | *I rode a camel in Egypt.* |
| past participle: | *Have you ever ridden a motorcycle?* (not *rode!*) |

### 2.2.14 *run/ran/run*

present:           *I <u>run</u> 10 miles every day.*
past:               *Sofia <u>ran</u> for the bus.* (not *run!*)
past participle: *They've <u>run</u> this company for 25 years.* (not *ran!*)

### 2.2.15 *sink/sank/sunk*

This is another very common mistake. It's the past tense that people often get wrong.

wrong:    *The Titanic <u>sunk</u> in 1912.*
right:      *The Titanic <u>sank</u> in 1912.*

present:           *Uh oh! We're in the Bermuda Triangle. I hope we don't <u>sink</u>.*
past:               *The ship <u>sank</u> after it was hit by a torpedo.* (not *sunk!*)
past participle: *Many ships have <u>sunk</u> in these dangerous waters.* (not *sank!*)

### 2.2.16 *see/saw/seen*

WARNING!!! *I seen* is a very common mistake and makes you sound like a bumpkin, so watch it!

present:           *Look! I <u>see</u> a monster.*
past:               *Carlos <u>saw</u> a ghost last night.* (not *seen!*)
past participle: *I have never <u>seen</u> that movie.*

### 2.2.17 *shake/shook/shaken*

present:           <u>*Shake*</u> *this salad dressing before you open the bottle.*
past:               *The earthquake <u>shook</u> the city.*
past participle: *I was <u>shaken</u> by the news.* (not *shook!*)

### 2.2.18 *sneak/sneaked/sneaked*

The ghastly abomination *snuck* has sneaked into the English language in recent years, but no matter how common it has, sadly, become, it's still wrong. Resist! Use the correct past form and past participle, *sneaked*.

present:           *Let's <u>sneak</u> into the movie theater.*
past:               *The student <u>sneaked</u> out of the classroom.* (not *snuck!*)
past participle: *My son has <u>sneaked</u> out of the house.* (not *snuck!*)

### 2.2.19 *swing/swung/swung*

present:           *The children like to <u>swing</u> in the backyard.*
past:               *The parachutist <u>swung</u> from the tree for hours before he was rescued.* (not *swang!*)
past participle: *He might have <u>swung</u> from the tree forever if he hadn't had his cell phone.*

### 2.2.20 *take/took/taken*

present:           *I usually <u>take</u> the 6:42 train in the morning.*
past:               *My wife <u>took</u> my dog when she left me.*

past participle:    *I wish I hadn't <u>taken</u> so long to call the fire department.* (not *took* or *tooken!*)

### 2.2.21 *tear/tore/torn*

present:            *Be careful. You might <u>tear</u> your pants.*
past:               *I <u>tore</u> up the paper and threw it away.*
past participle:    *Oh no! I've <u>torn</u> my shirt.* (not *tore!*)
adjective:          *I'm all <u>torn</u> up.* (not *tore!*)

### 2.2.22 *throw/threw/thrown*

present:            *I think I might <u>throw</u> up.*
past:               *Larry <u>threw</u> the ball to Emily.* (not *throwed!*)
past participle:    *Have you <u>thrown</u> out the garbage?* (not *throwed!*)

### 2.2.23 *write/wrote/written*

present:            *Every day I <u>write</u> a list of things to do.*
past:               *He <u>wrote</u> an email to his sister yesterday.*
past participle:    *I've <u>written</u> nine books.* (not *wrote!*)

## Quiz 2.2.1-2.2.23

Each of these sentences has an error. Find it and correct it.

1. There was a gas leak, and the house blowed up.

2. I can't use my printer. It's broke.

3. He come here last week, but I didn't see him.

4. He has came here many times.

5. The police think David may have did it.

6. I drug his body to the river and throwed him in.

7. Lisa's boyfriend has drank all her beer.

8. Have you ever went to Disney World?

9. I was sick yesterday, so I just laid in bed and watched TV.

10. Have you just been laying there all day?

11. You've laid there all day watching TV. Get up, you bum!

12. I've never rode a motorcycle.

13. I haven't ran so fast since the last time Godzilla attacked.

14. The boat sunk after it sprang a leak.

15. I seen it with my own eyes.

16. We were all shook by the news.

17. The class was so boring that I snuck out of the classroom.

18. He was all tore up when he learned of the tragedy.

19. My mother throwed out all my baseball cards.

20. He's wrote to her many times, but she never answers.

# 2.3 • Words Frequently Confused with Other Words

### 2.3.1 *advance* or *advanced*?
Use *advance* to describe something that happens ahead of time.

> *I had no advance warning of the layoffs.*
> *Did she make a reservation in advance?*

Use *advanced* to talk about something at a higher level, more complex, more difficult.

> *My son is taking an advanced calculus course.*
> *Many English teacher don't understand advanced grammar.*

### 2.3.2 *adverse* or *averse*?
Both refer to something bad, but a common mistake is to use *adverse* when *averse* is what's needed.

*Adverse* refers to something harmful, unfavorable, troublesome or problematic.

> *I had an adverse reaction to some medicine I was taking.*
> *The 15-car accident was blamed on adverse driving conditions.*

*Averse* describes an attitude of reluctance, hesitance, dislike or opposition.

> *Anna is averse to buying cosmetics that are tested on animals.*
> *I am averse to lending my brother-in-law money.*

It might help to remember that the adjective *averse* is related to the noun *aversion*. The examples above could be paraphrased as

> *Anna has an aversion to buying cosmetics that are tested on animals.*
> *I have an aversion to lending my brother-in-law money.*

### 2.3.3 *affect* or *effect*?
*Affect* is a verb. *Effect* is a noun. When you *affect* something, the result is the *effect*.

> *Did the price increase affect sales?*
> *I warned the student that skipping class would negatively affect his grades.*

> *The new law had no effect on the crime late.*
> *The experimental medicine had some undesirable effects.*

Just to complicate matters, *effect* is sometimes, though rarely, used as a verb. It means *to bring about something*.

> The new owners tried to <u>*effect*</u> *several changes in the employees' attitudes and behaviors.*

### 2.3.4 *alternate* or *alternative*?
*Alternate* is a verb meaning to switch back and forth from one option to the other.

> *My wife and I have only one set of chop sticks, so when we eat Chinese food, we have to <u>alternate</u>.*

*Alternative* is a noun meaning instead of the other or someone or something that substitutes.

> *There's only one course of action that makes any sense. There's no <u>alternative</u>.*

### 2.3.5 *among* or *between*?
*Between* is used only when talking about two things. Otherwise, use *among*.

> *The teacher was standing <u>between</u> Larry and Emily.*
> *This is a picture of my father standing <u>among</u> his parents and siblings.*

### 2.3.6 *amount* or *number*?
*Amount* is used for things that we don't count, *number* for things that we do count. A common mistake is to use *amount* when *number* is correct.

> *There was a large <u>amount</u> of blood on the floor.*
> *Most people have no idea of the <u>amount</u> of sugar in soft drinks.*
>
> *A large <u>number</u> of people were arrested at the protests.*
> *The <u>number</u> of customers declined after the food poisoning incident.*

### 2.3.7 *anxious* or *eager*?
People often confuse these. They are not the same.

*Anxious* is an adjective that implies, not surprisingly, anxiety, and anxiety is a bad thing, right?

*Eager* is an adjective that implies enthusiasm, and enthusiasm is a good thing, right?

It's when *to* is added that people get into trouble. When you are excited about doing something in the future, you are *eager to* do it. *Anxious to* doesn't make sense. You're *anxious about* something in the future that you dread, that you're nervous about.

> *I am <u>eager to</u> leave on my round-the-world vacation, but I'm <u>anxious about</u> the cost.*

### 2.3.8 *allude* or *refer*?
When you *refer to* something, you name it. You are unambiguous and direct. When you *allude to* something, you are indirect. You are suggesting without explicitly naming. You are depending on your listener or reader to figure out your true meaning.

> *When he mentioned my worthless brother, he was <u>referring to</u> Tom, not Jim.*
> *When he talked about my colorful past, he was <u>alluding to</u> my murder conviction.*

### 2.3.9 *appraise* or *apprise*?

*Appraise* means to determine the value of something. *Apprise* means to inform people of important information.

> *The jeweler <u>appraised</u> my mother's diamond ring.*
> *The doctor <u>apprised</u> me of my grandfather's condition.*

### 2.3.10 *assume* or *presume*?

These are not the same. *Assume* means to come to a conclusion based on facts or feelings. You might be right; you might be wrong, but that's what you think.

> *The new manager grew up in Japan, so I <u>assume</u> he speaks Japanese.*

*Presume* means to overdo it with your assumption. It implies an element of audacity.

> *I'm a gourmet chef and my son-in-law, because he used to work at Burger King, <u>presumes</u> to tell me how to cook.*

When you *presume*, you are *presumptuous*.

### 2.3.11 *assure* or *ensure* or *insure*?

All have similar meanings. *Assure* means to try to give people confidence or remove doubts. *Ensure* and *insure* both mean to make sure something happens. *Insure* is more common, and only *insure* is used in reference to insurance.

### 2.3.12 *bazaar* or *bizarre*?

A *bazaar* is a market. *Bizarre* is an adjective meaning *very strange*. Although these words sound similar, there is no connection, but of course a strange market would be a bizarre bazaar.

### 2.3.13 *bemused* or *amused*?

*Amused*, of course, means to be find something funny. *Bemused* has nothing to do with being amused or humor at all. It means *bewildered, confused, puzzled*. It's how members of the Grammar Police feel when they hear people say *I could care less* even though it so obviously doesn't make sense.

### 2.3.14 *beside* or *besides*?

*Beside* means apart from, next to or at the side of. A common mistake is to use *besides* when *beside* is correct.

> *The man I sat <u>beside</u> on the flight would not shut up.*

*Besides* means in addition to or moreover.

> *Who came to the party <u>besides</u> Larry and Emily?*
> *I don't want to go to that restaurant. Their food is terrible, and <u>besides</u>, I'm not hungry.*

### 2.3.15 *cache* or *cachet*?

A *cache* (pronounced like *cash*) is a store of something (often hidden) that has been set aside for use at a later time. We can talk of a cache of weapons or a cache of food or other supplies.

*Cachet* (pronounced *cashAY,* with a silent *t*) is an adjective that refers to a quality of prestige or status that a person, place or thing (like a brand) might have.

### 2.3.16 *capital* or *capitol*?
The city which is the center of government of a certain region or country is the *capital.* The building in which legislators meet is the *capitol.*

### 2.3.17 *cavalry* or *calvary*?
In the past, *cavalry* referred to soldiers on horses but is used today to refer also to highly mobile soldiers in vehicles or helicopters.

*Calvary* is where Christians believe Jesus was crucified.

### 2.3.18 *censure* or *censor*?
*Censure* (pronounced *SENshur*) is to criticize harshly or express severe disapproval. *Censor* is to hide or suppress information.

### 2.3.19 *compare* or *contrast*?
The Grammar Police maintain that *compare* is properly used to discuss similarities and *contrast* to discuss differences. Personally, I maintain that *compare* is often used for both and that this is not something anyone should worry about. If, for example, your friend asks you to compare your old job and your new job, and you discuss some ways that they are different, I think it's pretty unlikely that he'll object and say that he asked you only to compare them and not to contrast them. If he does, he's a jerk who should be shunned. Still, it's good to know the distinction just in case. Here's an example of how *compare* is used to liken one thing to another from a different class. Notice that I'm using *compare to.*

> He <u>compared</u> her hair <u>to</u> spun gold and her smile <u>to</u> rays of sunshine.

To further complicate this murky business, *compare with* is used when the differences between two members of the same class are more important than the similarities. That's how most people use *compare.*

So what does it boil down to? If you're writing poems, songs or love letters, use *compare to.* If you're using *compare* the way it's usually used, use *compare with* rather than *compare to,* and if you're really focused solely on differences, use *contrast with.*

### 2.3.20 *complement* or *compliment*?
*Compliment* is what you want when you're talking about saying nice things about someone or something.

> Sarah <u>complimented</u> me on my apple pie.

*Complement* comes from *complete.* If one thing complements another, it matches it, goes nicely with it or the two make a good combination.

> The russet-colored shade of the carpet <u>complements</u> the rustic décor and furnishings.
> Their personalities <u>complement</u> each other.

### 2.3.21 *continual* or *continuous*?

When something is *continuous,* it never stops.

*The Earth's rotation around the sun is <u>continuous</u>.*

When something is *continual,* it occurs frequently but intermittently. It is not nonstop.

*My wife's <u>continual</u> complaining is driving me crazy.*

The same applies to *continually* and *continuously.*

*My neighbors <u>continually</u> play loud music.*
*It's been raining <u>continuously</u> for three days. It hasn't stopped for a minute.*

### 2.3.22 *convince* or *persuade*?

The mistake that many people make with these two is using *convince* when *persuade* is correct. Here's what it boils down to: You *convince* people or you *convince* people *of* something

*I <u>convinced</u> the committee that my plan is superior.*
*I <u>convinced</u> the committee that my plan is superior. (that is optional)*
*I <u>convinced</u> the committee <u>of</u> the superiority of my plan.*

but you *persuade* people *to do* something.

*I <u>persuaded</u> the committee <u>to</u> adopt my plan.*

### 2.3.23 *council* or *counsel*?

*Council* is a noun meaning a meeting or organization created for some purpose.

*Counsel* is a verb meaning to advise. That's what *counselors* do—give advice. *Counsel* can also be used as noun meaning the advice itself or the person giving that advice.

### 2.3.24 *cue* or *queue*?

These words are pronounced exactly the same, like the letter *q.*

*Cue* is a reminder or signal for someone to do something. A *queue* is a line of people. *Queue up* is a verb, common in British English but seldom used in American English, meaning *line up.*

### 2.3.25 *discreet* or *discrete*?

These words have a common origin and are pronounced the same, but the meanings are different. When you're *discreet,* you keep a low profile and are careful about what you say—you use *discretion. Discrete* means separate, distinct, detached, unrelated.

### 2.3.26 *uninterested* or *disinterested*?

These are not the same. *Uninterested* means just what you think it means: not interested in something.

*I'm <u>uninterested</u> in sports.*

But *disinterested* means neutral, not involved, impartial, unbiased, not influenced by feelings or personal involvement.

> *A <u>disinterested</u> party was chosen to negotiate a settlement between the two warring factions.*

### 2.3.27 *emigrate* or *immigrate*?

*Emigrate* means to leave a country to live in another country. *Immigrate* means to come from another country to live. They seem kind of the same, don't they? It really depends on which you're focusing on—coming or going.

### 2.3.28 *enormousness* or *enormity*?

*Enormousness,* of course, comes from *enormous.* It refers to the massive size of something.

> *When I flew from Los Angeles to Tokyo, I was amazed by the <u>enormousness</u> of the Pacific Ocean.*

*Enormity* does not refer to bigness, and using it for bigness is the mistake that many people make. It refers to the outrageousness or the wickedness of something.

> *Even veteran detectives were shocked by the <u>enormity</u> of the crime.*

### 2.3.29 *entitle* or *title*?

People are *entitled,* For example,

> *You're <u>entitled</u> to three weeks of vacation after you've worked here for five years.*

Books, movies, articles, etc., are *titled.*

> wrong: *The movie is <u>entitled</u> Zombies Ate My Brain.*
> right: *The movie is <u>titled</u> Zombies Ate My Brain.*

### 2.3.30 *exasperate* or *exacerbate*?

People often confuse these words, generally using *exasperate* when *exacerbate* is needed. *Exasperate* means to irritate or annoy to a high degree. *Exacerbate* means to make a situation worse or to increase the severity of something. So, if you try to help your friends with their marriage problems and end up making things worse, you *exacerbated* the situation.

### 2.3.31 *farther* or *further*?

*Farther* and *further* are not the same. Both can be used when talking about distance.

> *How much <u>farther</u> are we going to drive?*
> *How much <u>further</u> are we going to drive?*

But when talking about doing something to a greater degree or extent, use *further.* Keep in mind that it's related to *furthermore.*

> *I pointed out why Plan A was bad and <u>further</u> pointed out why Plan B is better. There's no need for you to explain any <u>further</u>. I get it.*

### 2.3.32 *flare* or *flair*?

*Flare* is about fire or conflict. Tempers can *flare,* fires can *flare up,* solar flares can burn the Earth to a lifeless, smoldering lump of rubble. *Flair* is about style or talent. You can dress with *flair* or have a natural *flair* for drawing.

### 2.3.33 *flout* or *flaunt*?

WARNING!!! Confusing these is a common mistake that the Grammar Police can spot a mile away. When you willingly ignore or violate rules, conventions or traditions, you *flout* them.

> *He's the boss's son, so he can <u>flout</u> the rules.*

When you *flaunt* something, you're showing off.

> *He's rich, but he doesn't <u>flaunt</u> it. He lives in a small house and drives an old car.*

### 2.3.34 *forward* or *foreword*?

*Forward* is about direction. That's easy, but a written passage at the beginning of a book is a *foreword.*

### 2.3.35 *gantlet* or *gauntlet*?

*Gantlet* is a Swedish word for lane. *Running the gantlet* referred to the practice of punishing someone by forcing him to run between two rows of men who would hit him with clubs. Nowadays we use it metaphorically to mean having to endure harsh criticism from several sources.

A *gauntlet* was the armored glove worn by a knight. To challenge an opponent, he would throw it on the ground in front of the person he wanted to challenge. We still use *throw down the gauntlet* to mean *offer a challenge,* but rarely is armor involved.

The mistake many make is using *gauntlet* when *gantlet* is required. Some maintain that this has become acceptable, but the Grammar Police disapprove, so try to keep them straight.

### 2.3.36 *grizzly* or *grisly*?

*Grizzly* is the name of a large North American bear. *Grisly* (pronounced the same a *grizzly*) is an adjective meaning horrible in a bloody sort of way—a *grisly* crime, a *grisly* massacre. If you were attacked by a grizzly bear, the people on the trail behind you would come upon a grisly scene.

### 2.3.37 *healthy* or *healthful*?

This is really a lost cause, but there are people who still maintain the distinction between *healthy* and *healthful.* To them (and to me), talking about *healthy food* sounds really...well, dumb. What it boils down to is that living things are or are not *healthy,* and what they eat is or is not *healthful.* Just remember this:

> *I'm <u>healthy</u> because I eat <u>healthful</u> food.*

### 2.3.38 *homey* or *homely*?

Does *homely* mean plain, unattractive or ugly, or does it mean cozy and comfortable, often used to describe a house? Well, it means both depending on which side of the Atlantic you are on. In US English, *homely* has come to mean plain, unattractive or ugly whereas in British English, *homely* means comfortable and cozy. *Homey* is what is used for comfortable and cozy in US English. So what to do? If there's any danger of misunderstanding, avoid *homely* entirely.

### 2.3.39 *home in* or *hone in*?

*Home in* means to get closer to your goal. *Hone* means to sharpen your skills. Many confuse these and speak of *honing in* on a goal. Don't you be one of them. Say *home in*.

### 2.3.40 *illusion* or *delusion*?

An *illusion* is false perception or belief, like a mirage or an optical illusion or a situation where something or someone pretends to be something or someone else. This false perception is the result of something external that is not what it appears to be. A *delusion* is a false perception or belief caused by internal psychological factors.

### 2.3.41 *imply* or *infer*?

Many people confuse these, usually using *infer* when *imply* is correct. *Imply* is to say something without actually saying it.

> *When you say it's too complicated to explain, are you <u>implying</u> that I'm not smart enough to understand?*

*Infer* is reading between the lines—to understand what someone is saying without saying it.

> *When the boss said the company needs to start cutting back in view of our poor sales, I <u>inferred</u> that I might lose my job.*

### 2.3.42 *irritate* or *aggravate*?

Many people confuse these, and it really aggravates me. Actually, that was an example of the mistake many people make. *Irritate* means annoy.

> *My neighbors play loud music all night, and it really <u>irritates</u> me.*

*Aggravate* means to make a situation worse.

> *I <u>aggravated</u> my bad knee playing football yesterday.*

### 2.3.43 *jive* or *jibe*?

Do you say that something doesn't *jive with the facts*? If you do, stop! *Jive* is a term used to describe jazz or acting in jazzy manner. If you're talking about something not being consistent with something else, *jibe with* is what you want.

> *His alibi doesn't <u>jibe with</u> the facts.*

### 2.3.44 *lend* or *loan*?

Strictly speaking, *lend* is verb, and *loan* is a noun. Using *loan* as a verb, although very common, is frowned upon by the Grammar Police.

frowned upon by the Grammar Police:   *I loaned my brother $100.*
better:                               *I lent my brother $100.*

## 2.3.45 *lay low* or *lie low*?

WARNING!!! *Lay* and *lie* are very commonly confused, and doing so is considered a major felony by the Grammar Police, so do not fail to see my discussion of both of these verbs in 2.2.10 and 2.2.11.

really, really wrong:   *The police are looking for me. I need to lay low.*
right:                 *The police are looking for me. I need to lie low.*

## 2.3.46 *loath* or *loathe*?

*Loath* is an adjective meaning reluctant to do something. (The *th* sounds like the *th* in *both*.)

*I got food poisoning last time I ate at Joe's Diner, so I am loath to eat there again.*

*Loathe* is a verb. It means hate. (The *th* sounds like the *th* in *breathe*.)

*I loathe my daughter's husband.*

## 2.3.47 *loose* or *lose*?

*Loose* is an adjective, the opposite of tight. It rhymes with *goose*. *Lose* is a verb, the opposite of win and find. It rhymes with *news*.

## 2.3.48 *nauseous* or *nauseated*?

Most people nowadays would say that they're *nauseous* when they feel queasy and likely to vomit. Some members of the Grammar Police are willing to accept this, but other, more strict members, insist that *nauseous* means something disgusting that makes people feel *nauseated*.

*The filthy toilet was nauseous. It made me feel nauseated.*

## 2.3.49 *notorious* or *famous*?

Many people think *notorious* means *famous,* and they're right, sort of. *Notorious* does mean famous, however, it means famous for something bad. The same is true of *notoriety*. So, if you're notorious, you need to change your ways.

## 2.3.50 *passed* or *past*?

*Pass* is a verb. The past form and past participle are both *passed*.

*I passed the slow-moving car.*
*A lot of time has passed.*

Using *past* as a verb is not correct.

*Past* is a noun.

*He lives in the past.*

It's a preposition.

*It's past midnight.*

It's an adjective.

*My best days are <u>past</u>.*

And it's an adverb.

*We drove <u>past</u> Larry's house.*

### 2.3.51 *phaze* or *faze*?

*Phase* is a noun meaning a temporary condition or situation or stage in a longer process.

*She's going through a <u>phase</u>.*

and a verb meaning to a change gradually

*We're going to <u>phase</u> in the new payroll system in stages.*

but when you want to say that something upset your composure or irritated or intimidated you, the word you want is *faze*. It's almost always used in negative sentences. (See 2.3.66 for a discussion of *unphased* and *unfazed*.)

*I knew I was the right man for the job, so the long interview process didn't <u>faze</u> me. The coach wasn't <u>fazed</u> by the team's 72-0 loss.*

### 2.3.52 *pique, peak* or *peek*?

Is this book *peaking* your interest in proper English? I hope not. I'd much rather it were *piquing* your interest. This is a very common mistake. *Peak* means the top of a mountain, high above. When you're interest in something is heightened, it seems logical to say it has *peaked* your interest—logical but wrong. *Pique* is a verb meaning to excite, either in a good way, as something interesting might do, or a bad way, as something upsetting might do. Something that *piques* your interest excites you intellectually.

*Pique* can also be used as a noun meaning *annoyance*. If you're in a *fit of pique*, you're annoyed or indignant, especially because you feel you haven't been treated with respect.

And don't confuse *pique* with *peek*, to have quick look at something, either.

### 2.3.53 *pore* or *pour*?

*Pour* means just what you think it means. You do it with liquids: pour a cup of coffee, etc.

But when you study or look over a map, plan or some printed material in a very thorough way, you *pore over* it. I hope you are *poring over* this book.

### 2.3.54 *prescribe* or *proscribe*?

When you *prescribe*, you tell people what they should do.

*The doctor <u>prescribed</u> antibiotics.*

When you *proscribe*, you prohibit something or tell people what they should not do.

*The Grammar Police have <u>proscribed</u> snuck and <u>prescribed</u> sneaked.*

### 2.3.55 *principle* or *principal*?

*Principle* is a noun meaning a fundamental belief or a scientific law. *Principal* is an adjective meaning primary or main and a noun meaning the head of a school.

### 2.3.56 *prostate* or *prostrate*?

The *prostate* is an organ that males have. One speaks of *prostate cancer*. *Prostrate* is an adjective meaning to lie face down on the ground.

### 2.3.57 *quote* or *quotation*?

This is sort of a lost cause, but if you want to impress your friends and neighbors and avoid disapproving glances from the Grammar Police, use *quote* only as a verb and *quotation* as a noun.

| | |
|---|---|
| correct use of *quote*: | *Our boss is a moron, but don't <u>quote</u> me on that.* |
| incorrect use of *quote*: | *"If you're going through hell, keep going" is a famous <u>quote</u> by Winston Churchill.* |
| correct use of *quotation*: | *"If you're going through hell, keep going" is a famous <u>quotation</u> by Winston Churchill.* |

### 2.3.58 *rack* or *wrack*?

These words are often confused, and for members of the Grammar Police, it can be *nerve-racking*. Here's what it boils down to: In medieval times, when you *racked* someone, you tortured him or her on a *rack*. This tortuous experience is why we say *nerve-racking* and *rack your brain*.

*Wrack* is an old-fashioned variation of *wreck*, and that's why we say *wrack and ruin, storm-wracked, guilt-wracked, wracked with guilt, pain-wracked* and *wracked with pain*.

Regarding whether *wrack* or *rack* should be used in *storm-wracked, guilt-wracked, wracked with guilt, pain-wracked* and *wracked with pain*, etc., there is much disagreement and no clear answer, so the advice often given is that either *rack* or *wrack* is acceptable—rare flexibility from the Grammar Police.

### 2.3.59 *ravage* or *ravish*?

*Ravish* means *to overwhelm in an emotional way*. The meaning is similar to entrance, enrapture or enchant. It can also mean to overwhelm in a sexual way. *Ravage* means to severely damage.

### 2.3.60 *rain, reign* or *rein*?

WARNING!!! These are all pronounced the same way, but using the wrong one when you write, a very common mistake, can make you look dumb.

*Rain,* of course, is water falling from the sky.

*Reign,* which is a verb and a noun, refers to the span of a monarch's rule. Queen Victoria's *reign* lasted from 1837 to 1901. She *reigned* from 1837 to 1901. So that's the word you want when you speak of a *reign of terror.*

| dumb: | *Hitler's <u>rain</u> of terror ended in 1945.* |
|---|---|
| correct: | *Hitler's <u>reign</u> of terror ended in 1945.* |

*Reins* are the leather straps that are attached to a horse's bit. Giving a horse *free rein* means holding the reins loosely so it can move freely. Metaphorically, therefore, giving someone free rein means giving him or her freedom to do whatever he or she wants.

| dumb: | *The CEO gave the new VP free <u>rain</u> to reorganize the sales department.* |
|---|---|
| dumb: | *The CEO gave the new VP free <u>reign</u> to reorganize the sales department.* |
| correct: | *The CEO gave the new VP free <u>rein</u> to reorganize the sales department.* |

## 2.3.61 *sight, site* or *cite*?

A *sight,* of course, is something to see or the ability to see. A *site* is a place or location, for example, a building site or an archaeological site. A *web site,* therefore, is a place on the Internet. *Web sight* is a common mistake; only *web site* is correct. Making this mistake will make you look dumb, so don't make it.

*Cite* means to identify the source of information. It's often used in academic writing.

## 2.3.62 *stanch* or *staunch*?

Have you ever cut off one of your arms or legs and had difficulty *staunching* the bleeding? If so, then you made a common mistake: confusing *stanch* and *staunch.* The verb *stanch* means to stop the flow of something, usually bleeding. So next time you cut yourself, good luck *stanching* the bleeding.

The adjective *staunch* means being strong in support of one's beliefs or principles.

*I am a <u>staunch</u> supporter of women's rights.*

## 2.3.63 *stationary* or *stationery*?

*Stationary* means immobile, fixed in place. Something *stationary* stays is one place. *Stationery* is writing paper.

## 2.3.64 *they're, their* or *there*?

It's very easy to confuse these. I do it myself when I type faster than I think (which isn't very fast). I don't think there's any need to explain what they mean. The main thing is to be careful because using the wrong one looks careless and sloppy.

## 2.3.65 *to, too* or *two*?

Just like *they're, their* and *there,* it's very easy to confuse *to, too* and *two.* Again, the main thing is to be careful because using the wrong one looks careless and sloppy.

## 2.3.66 *unphased* or *unfazed*?

This is a very common mistake. *Unphased* is a technical term. *Unfazed* is the word you want when you mean calm, unbothered, untroubled, not deterred. (See 2.3.51 for a discussion of *phase* and *faze*.)

| wrong: | *I was <u>unphazed</u> by his criticism.* |
|---|---|
| right: | *I was <u>unfazed</u> by his criticism.* |

### 2.3.67 *weather* or *whether*?

When you're talking about rain, snow, clouds, sunshine and the like, you're talking about *weather*. Don't confuse it with *whether*, as in *Sadly, many people don't care whether they use correct English.*

### 2.3.68 *whose* or *who's*?

WARNING!!! Many people spell *whose*, as in *Whose car is this?* as *who's*, the contraction of *who is*, as in *Who's he?*, and *who has*, as in *Who's seen that movie?* This can make you look dumb, so try to get this right.

### 2.3.69 *your* or *you're*?

WARNING!!! Confusing *your* and *you're* is a very common mistake and will make you look dumb, so don't do it!

## Quiz 2.3.1-2.3.69

Each of these sentences has an error (or can be improved). Find it and correct it.

1. Our hospital has the most advance medical technology.

2. Some believe that the US had advanced knowledge of the Pearl Harbor attack.

3. Lisa's shy and adverse to being the center of attention.

4. My application got lost between the other 20 applications.

5. What amount of guests are coming to your wedding?

6. We're really anxious to go on vacation next month.

7. The caller asked for Bob, but I didn't know if he was alluding to Bob Jr. or Bob Sr.

8. The boss asked me to appraise him of the problems at the Nashville office.

9. Larry's flight to Chicago left six hours ago. Since it's a three-hour flight, I presume he's in Chicago now.

10. We got cheated at a bizarre in Istanbul.

11. This doesn't make any sense at all. It's really bazaar.

12. I was not bemused by his stupid jokes.

13. I have no family beside my sister.

14. The explorers left a cachet of food for the return journey.

15. People pay high prices for Rolex watches mainly because the name has a certain cache.

16. The capitol of Illinois is Springfield.

17. The state's capital building was completed in 1868.

18. In many countries, the government censures the Internet.

19. The senator was censored for his racist comments.

20. Yesterday, my teacher complemented me on how good my report was.

21. The woman at the cosmetics counter said this shade of lip stick would compliment my eye color.

22. The factory operates 24/7. Production is continual.

23. I didn't want to go to the ballet, but my wife convinced me to go.

24. Members of the counsel voted in favor of the agreement.

25. My parents counciled me not to major in philosophy, but I didn't listen.

26. There was a long cue at the British Museum.

27. When David passed out face first into a plate of spaghetti, that was my queue to close the bar.

28. The Internet and TV are no longer bundled. Now they are discreet services.

29. Don't tell my sister anything. She's incapable of being discrete.

30. Lisa thinks I'm boring. She's disinterested in anything I say.

31. When I moved to Alaska from Rhode Island, I was amazed at the enormity of the state.

32. When my parents were killed, I was overwhelmed by the enormousness of my loss.

33. Margaret Mitchell's only book was entitled *Gone with the Wind.*

34. Just leave well enough alone. If you do anything, it will just exasperate the situation.

35. The farther I investigate this matter, the more shocked I become.

36. My daughter has a flare for music.

37. They thought the forest fire was out, but then it flaired up again.

38. Did you see how Mary was flouting her new engagement ring at work today?

39. Many young people flaunt society's conventions.

40. I asked Professor Davis to write a forward for my book.

41. It was a grizzly crime scene.

42. Sadly, David learned that grisly bears aren't as cuddly as he thought.

43. After I adopted a healthy diet, I lost weight and felt a lot better.

44. My sister isn't healthful. She's in the hospital again.

45. The missile honed in on the target and totally destroyed it.

46. I was sure the pink elephant was real, but it was only an alcohol-induced illusion.

47. What was your sister inferring when she commented that I used to be so thin?

48. When the HR guy suggested I update my résumé, I implied that I was going to be laid off soon.

49. It really aggravates me when you never let me finish a sentence.

50. My brother-in-law asked me to loan him my lawn mower.

51. I absolutely loath public speaking.

52. After what happened last time, my sister is loathe to ever invite her mother-in-law to another dinner party.

53. One of my students has several screws lose.

54. If we loose this game, we have no chance of making it to the finals.

55. I felt nauseous when I saw the crime scene photos.

56. The doctor was notorious for treating poor people at no charge.

57. Carlos wasn't in the least bit phased by the enormous challenge he faced.

58. It's passed 8:00, so that means we're late for work.

59. Larry past the ball to Francesca.

60. I took a peak at my brother's photos of mountain peeks, and it peaked my interest in mountain climbing.

61. The pathetic member of the Grammar Police pours over grammar books all day long.

62. Your doctor may proscribe creams and ointments that you should use for your psoriasis.

63. There are laws which prescribe discrimination based on race and gender.

64. The principle wants me to come to his office after class.

65. Separation of powers is a fundamental principal of American democracy.

66. One of my favorite quotes is "If you want to make God laugh, tell him about your plans."

67. I gave the interior decorator free reign to do anything she wanted.

68. Edward VI reined for only six years.

69. The company created a new web sight.

70. The developers chose a cite for the new mall.

71. At the meeting, the CEO sited poor customer service as the main reason that revenue had dropped in recent years.

72. When I cut off my toe while chopping wood, it took forever to staunch the bleeding.

73. I exercise on a stationery bicycle.

74. We went to a stationary store to buy some paper and pens.

75. There car is over their, next to mine.

76. I don't want to go outside. It's to hot.

77. Do you know weather or not the whether guy is forecasting rain?

78. The man who's car was stolen had to take the bus to work.

79. Do you know whose going to the meeting?

80. Your really starting to make me angry!

# 2.4 • One Word or Two?

## 2.4.1 *alot* or *a lot*?
A lot of people make this mistake.

| | |
|---|---|
| no such word: | *alot* |
| correct: | *a lot* |

## 2.4.2 *already* or *all ready*?
It depends. *Already* is an adverb meaning before a certain time. *All ready* can mean totally ready or that everyone or everything is ready.

*I'm not hungry because I've <u>already</u> eaten.*

but

*My wife isn't ready to go yet, but I'm <u>all ready</u>.*
*Every one of my students is ready for the test. They're <u>all ready</u>.*

### 2.4.3 *alright* or *all right*?

It's not *all right* to use *alright*.

   no such word:   *alright*
   correct:         *all right*

### 2.4.4 *altogether* or *all together*?

It depends. *Altogether* is an adverb meaning *entirely* or *in total*.

> *Altogether*, *she takes seven different medications every day for her various ailments.*
> *I had to give up tennis* *altogether* *after my hip surgery.*

but

> *It's nice to have our entire family* *all together* *for Christmas.*

### 2.4.5 *anymore* or *any more*?

It depends.

> *I don't live in the city* *anymore*. *I moved to the suburbs.*

but

> *We're out of coffee. We don't have* *any more* *coffee.*

### 2.4.6 *anyone* or *any one*?

*Anyone,* when it has the same meaning as *anybody,* is one word.

> *This is secret. Don't tell* *anyone*.

But don't use *anyone* when you're talking about any member of a group.

   wrong:   *They're all the same. You can take* *anyone* *of them.*
   right:    *They're all the same. You can take* *any one* *of them.*

### 2.4.7 *anyway* or *any way*?

You can do something *any way* you want to, but when you mean besides or in any case, it's *anyway.*

### 2.4.8 *awhile* or *a while*?

When you mean for a while, the adverb *awhile* has the same meaning.

> *Why don't you sit down and stay* *awhile*.

Otherwise, use *a while*.

> *David disappeared* *a while* *ago. We haven't seen him since.*

### 2.4.9 *everyday* or *every day*?

WARNING!!! When you're talking about something that's typical or ordinary, use the adjective *everyday.*

> *My* *everyday* *routine is to wake up, drink coffee, check my email and then take a shower.*

When you mean *each day,* use *every day.* Using *everyday* when *every day* is correct is a very common mistake that is easily noticed by the Grammar Police. You have been warned.

*I exercise <u>every day</u> except Sunday.*

### 2.4.10 *everyone* or *every one*?
*Everyone,* when it has the same meaning as *everybody,* is one word.

*My sister has a big mouth. She told <u>everyone</u>.*

But don't use *everyone* when you're talking about all members of a group.

*These are all defective. <u>Every one</u> of them needs to be replaced.*

## Quiz 2.4.1-2.4.10
Each of these sentences has an error. Find it and correct it.

1. Mary lost alot of money in Las Vegas.

2. I've all ready seen that movie. I don't want to see it again.

3. I'm already for my vacation.

4. There are no problems. Everything is alright.

5. All together, there were 42 people on the bus when it plunged into the gorge.

6. The boss wants the employees altogether to hear the announcement.

7. She's not married any more.

8. I'm all out of money. I don't have anymore.

9. I don't like anyone of my wife's relatives.

10. Did any one call while I was away?

11. I'm really tired. I need to rest a while.

12. It's been awhile since I last saw her.

13. Mass shootings are an every day event in the USA.

14. I drink coffee everyday.

15. I couldn't believe it when everyone of my students failed the test.

16. Sorry, I thought every one knew about the change of plan.

# 2.5 • Frequently Messed Up Phrases

### 2.5.1 *12 am/12 pm*
Did you know that there's no such thing as *12 am* or *12 pm*? Bet you didn't. *Am* doesn't actually start until 12:01:01 am, or in other words, one second after mid-

night. And *pm* doesn't actually start until 12:01:01 pm, or one second after noon. What??? (I know that's what you're thinking.) Here's what it boils down to: *Am* stands for *ante meridiem,* which is Latin for *before midday* (in other words, *before noon*) and *pm* stands for *post meridiem, after midday* (in other words, *after noon*). But when it's 12:00 (whether noon or midnight) it's neither before nor after.

Although it's traditional to refer to *12 am* as midnight and *12 pm* as noon, not everyone agrees, and this sometimes causes confusion, so to avoid confusion, and because these don't actually make sense, it's better to use *noon* and *midnight.* (And how's all this for a bit of trivia to amaze people with?)

### 2.5.2 *a mute point* or *a moot point*?

wrong:   *a mute point*
right:   *a moot point*

### 2.5.3 *all of the sudden* or *all of a sudden*?

wrong:   *all of the sudden*
right:   *all of a sudden*

### 2.5.4 *baited breath* or *bated breath*?

wrong:   *baited breath*
right:   *bated breath*

### 2.5.5 *beckon call* or *beck and call*?

wrong:   *beckon call*
right:   *beck and call*

### 2.5.6 *butt naked* or *buck naked*?

wrong:   *butt naked*
right:   *buck naked*

### 2.5.7 *buy in large* or *by and large*?

wrong:   *buy in large*
right:   *by and large*

### 2.5.8 *case and point* or *case in point*?

wrong:   *case and point*
right:   *case in point*

### 2.5.9 *chalk-full* or *chock-full*?

wrong:   *chalk-full*
right:   *chock-full*

## 2.5.10 *chock it up* or *chalk it up?*

wrong:  *chock it up*
right:  *chalk it up*

## 2.5.11 *chomping at the bit* or *champing at the bit?*
Many people say *chomping at the bit* because *chomp* seems like what a horse would do to something in its mouth, but the correct expression is *champing at the bit.*

wrong:  *chomping at the bit*
right:  *champing at the bit*

## 2.5.12 *consensus of opinion* or *consensus?*
Consensus refers to a collective opinion, so it's redundant to say *of opinion.*

wrong:  *consensus of opinion*
right:  *consensus*

## 2.5.13 *deep-seeded* or *deep-seated?*

wrong:  *deep-seeded*
right:  *deep-seated*

## 2.5.14 *do a 360* or *do a 180?*
There are 360 degrees in a circle, so if you *do a 360,* you're right back where you started from. If you mean you've completely changed your opinion to the opposite point of view, you *do a 180.*

wrong:  *do a 360*
right:  *do a 180*

## 2.5.15 *doggy-dog world* or *dog-eat-dog world?*

wrong:  *doggy-dog world*
right:  *dog-eat-dog world*

## 2.5.16 *ever so often* or *every so often?*
Some misguided wannabe members of the Grammar Police have twisted themselves into pretzels in order to explain why these are both correct but have opposite meanings. Don't believe them.

wrong:  *ever so often*
right:  *every so often*

## 2.5.17 *extract revenge* or *exact revenge?*
*Exact* can be used as a verb to mean demand or obtain.

wrong:  *extract revenge*
right:  *exact revenge*

## 2.5.18 *first come, first serve* or *first come, first served*?

wrong:  *first come, first <u>serve</u>*
right:   *first come, first <u>served</u>*

## 2.5.19 *for all intensive purposes* or *for all intents and purposes*?

wrong:  *for all <u>intensive</u> purposes*
right:   *for all <u>intents and</u> purposes*

## 2.5.20 *heart-wrenching* or *heart-rending*?

wrong:  *heart-<u>wrenching</u>*
right:   *heart-<u>rending</u>*

## 2.5.21 *I could care less* or *I couldn't care less*?
WARNING!!! Getting this wrong is one of the surest ways to cause the Grammar Police to snicker behind your back. Why? Because what is wrong is so obviously wrong that it makes people who know it's wrong wonder about the intelligence of anyone who cannot see that it's wrong. Here's what it boils down to: *I could care less* means that it <u>is</u> possible for you to care less because <u>you do care some</u>, but isn't that exactly the opposite of what people mean when they say this? Don't they mean that it is <u>impossible</u> for them to care less because <u>they do not care at all</u>? You have been warned.

wrong and dumb:  *I <u>could</u> care less.*
right:             *I <u>couldn't</u> care less.*

## 2.5.22 *if worse comes to worst* or *if worst comes to worst*?

wrong:  *if <u>worse</u> comes to <u>worst</u>*
right:   *if the <u>worst</u> comes to <u>worst</u>*

## 2.5.23 *make due* or *make do*?

wrong:  *make <u>due</u>*
right:   *make <u>do</u>*

## 2.5.24 *mano a mano*
Are you a tough guy who doesn't take any crap from anyone? Are you frank and direct, not afraid to speak your mind and talk to another guy who's giving you grief *mano a mano* to set him straight? *Man to man,* right? Wrong. The Spanish phrase *mano a mano* may look like *man to man,* but that's not what it means. *Mano* is *hand* in Spanish (*hombre* is *man*), so *mano a mano* means *hand in hand* and is used to refer to two people or entities either working together on an equal basis toward some common goal or competing on an equal basis. To anyone who speaks Spanish, which includes many members of the Grammar Police, using *mano a mano* for *man to man* sounds dumb, so don't do it. When you want to say *man to man,* here's a suggestion: say *man to man.*

### 2.5.25 *nape of the neck* or *nape*?

The human body has only one *nape*, so saying *nape of the neck* is redundant and wrong. Do you say *scalp of the head*, *tongue of the mouth*, *nose of the face* (I could go on)?

wrong:  *nape of the neck*
right:  *nape*

### 2.5.26 *nip it in the butt* or *nip it in the bud*?

If you remove a bud on a plant, that part of the plant can't continue to grow, so that's why we correctly say *nip it in the bud* to mean take some action to prevent a problem from getting worse.

wrong:  *nip it in the butt*
right:  *nip it in the bud*

### 2.5.27 *old adage* or *adage*?

An *adage* is a proverb or saying, something people have been saying for a long time. The idea of *old* is built into the word, so saying *old adage* is redundant and wrong.

wrong:  *old adage*
right:  *adage*

### 2.5.28 *on tenderhooks* or *on tenterhooks*?

*Tenterhooks* were hooks used to stretch wool cloth to prevent it from shrinking while it dried. The idea is that being in a state of anxiety is as unpleasant as being pierced and stretched with metal hooks.

wrong:  *on tenderhooks*
right:  *on tenterhooks*

### 2.5.29 *one in the same* or *one and the same*?

wrong:  *one in the same*
right:  *one and the same*

### 2.5.30 *physical year* or *fiscal year*?

wrong:  *physical year*
right:  *fiscal year*

### 2.5.31 *peak my interest* or *pique my interest*?

See the discussion of *pique, peak* and *peek* in 2.3.51.

wrong:  *peak my interest*
right:  *pique my interest*

### 2.5.32 *scott free* or *scot free*?

wrong:  *scott free*
right:  *scot free*

### 2.5.33 *shoe-in* or *shoo-in*?

wrong:   *shoe-in*
right:    *shoo-in*

### 2.5.34 *slight of hand* or *sleight of hand*?

wrong:   *slight of hand*
right:    *sleight of hand*

### 2.5.35 *sneak peak* or *sneak peek*?

wrong:   *sneak peak*
right:    *sneak peek*

### 2.5.36 *statue of limitations* or *statute of limitations*?

wrong:   *statue of limitations*
right:    *statute of limitations*

### 2.5.37 *surrounded on three sides*?

WARNING!!! If you're surrounded on two or three sides, you're not actually surrounded, are you? *Surrounded* means on all sides, so saying *surrounded on two* or *three sides* makes no sense. Be careful about this one. It's a particular pet peeve of many members of the Grammar Police. Say *bordered* instead.

### 2.5.38 *take a different tact* or *take a different track* or *take a different tack*?

*Tack* is a sailing term that means to change direction, so when you approach a situation or problem in a different way, you *take a different tack.*

wrong:   *take a different tact*
wrong:   *take a different track*
right:    *take a different tack*

### 2.5.39 *through the ringer* or *through the wringer*?

A *wringer* was an old-fashioned device with two rollers that people would put wet clothes through to squeeze the water out of them. Going *through the wringer* would be an unpleasant experience indeed.

wrong:   *through the ringer*
right:    *through the wringer*

### 2.5.40 *throws of passion* or *throes of passion*?

wrong:   *throws of passion*
right:    *throes of passion*

### 2.5.41 *tongue and cheek* or *tongue in cheek*?

wrong:   *tongue and cheek*
right:    *tongue in cheek*

### 2.5.42 *tow the line* or *toe the line*?

wrong:   *tow the line*
right:   *toe the line*

### 2.5.43 *without further adieu* or *without further ado*?

wrong:   *without further adieu*
right:   *without further ado*

### 2.5.44 *wet your appetite* or *whet your appetite*?

wrong:   *wet your appetite*
right:   *whet your appetite*

### 2.5.45 *worse-case scenario* or *worst-case scenario*?

wrong:   *worse-case scenario*
right:   *worst-case scenario*

### 2.5.46 *wreck havoc* or *wreak havoc*?

wrong:   *wreck havoc*
right:   *wreak havoc* (rhymes with *seek*)

### 2.5.47 *you've got another thing coming* or *you've got another think coming*?

wrong:   *You've got another thing coming.*
right:   *You've got another think coming.*

## Quiz 2.5.1-2.5.47
Each of these sentences has an error. Find it and correct it.

1. I worked on my project from 12 pm to 12 am.

2. It's a mute point.

3. And then, all of the sudden, her husband burst through the door.

4. Everyone waited with baited breath for the verdict.

5. Do it yourself. I'm not at your beckon call.

6. We were butt naked in the back seat of my car.

7. Buy in large, the students are pretty clueless.

8. Yesterday's incident is a good case and point.

9. The state that she comes from is chalk-full of wackos.

10. You can chock her win up to hours of training and a bit of luck.

11. I'm chomping at the bit to get started on this project.

12. The consensus of opinion is that the change was a big mistake.

13. We have some really deep-seeded problems in our society.

14. I did a 360 and changed my vote from yes to no on the referendum.

15. Be careful. It's a doggy-dog world out there.

16. Ever so often, one of my ideas actually works.

17. Someday I'll extract my revenge from that bastard.

18. After Lee surrendered, the Civil War was, for all intensive purposes, over.

19. You'd better hurry. It's first come, first serve.

20. It was a sad, heart-wrenching experience.

21. I could care less what he thinks about me.

22. If worse comes to worse, we can always eat our shoes.

23. We can't afford a new one. We'll just have to make due.

24. I've had it with that guy. I'm going to talk to him mano a mano and set him straight.

25. The pterodactyl picked me up by the nape of my neck.

26. We need to nip this in the butt before it gets any worse.

27. Remember the old adage, haste makes waste.

28. I've been on tenderhooks all week waiting for my exam results.

29. Chick peas and garbanzo beans are one in the same.

30. Our company's physical year runs from July 1 to June 30.

31. When he talked about Tahiti, it peaked my interest in going there.

32. I can't believe the murderer got off scott-free.

33. He's a shoe-in. He'll win with 90% of the votes.

34. There's going to be a sneak peak of the film before the premier tomorrow.

35. I'm not worried about being indicted. The statue of limitations has expired, so I'm safe.

36. My house is surrounded on three sides by the sea.

37. This isn't working. We need to take a different track.

38. My ex-wife really put me through the ringer.

39. His wife caught them in the throws of passion.

40. Don't pay any attention to him. It's all tongue and cheek.

41. Listen to me. You need to tow the line or get out!

42. Without further adieu, here is the star of the show.

43. Talking about my mother's favorite recipes really wet my appetite.

44. The worse-case scenario is that we'll all be eaten by piranhas.

45. That bull really wrecked havoc in my china shop.

# 2.6 • Problems with Pronunciation

Some words are so commonly mispronounced that, if you pronounce them correctly, people will think you've made a mistake. But if those people know you well, they won't think that because, if you've gotten this far in this book, you're already known and respected as someone who knows proper English and uses it. People will assume that whatever you say must be correct.

### 2.6.1 *accelerate*

wrong: *a•SEL•er•ate*
right: *ak•SEL•er•ate*

### 2.6.2 *accessible*

wrong: *a•SES•i•ble*
right: *ak•SES•i•ble*

### 2.6.3 *accessory*

wrong: *a•SES•or•y*
right: *ak•SES•or•y*

### 2.6.4 *ask*

wrong: *AKS*
right: *ASK*

### 2.6.5 *cache*

wrong: *cash•AY*
right: *cash*

### 2.6.6 *chaise longue*

Almost everyone gets *chaise longue* (as it's properly spelled) wrong. Amaze your friends and colleagues by getting it right! It's French for *long* (*longue*) *chair* (*chaise*). Since people relax and lounge on these long chairs, English speakers have turned *longue* into *lounge*, so this is a spelling thing too.

wrong:   *chase LOUNGE* (*chase lounge*)
right:     *shez LONG* (*chaise longue*)

### 2.6.7 *coup de grace*

Also French. Some people are vaguely aware that in French many final consonants are silent, so they incorrectly pronounce *grace* as *gra*. But not all final consonants in French are silent. The *p* in *coup* is silent, but not the *c* in *grace*.

wrong:   *koo da GRA*
right:     *koo da GRAS*

### 2.6.8 *divorcee*

wrong:   *di•VOR•see*
right:     *di•vor•SAY*

### 2.6.9 *err*

Many people err when they pronounce *err,* and those people will look at you funny when you pronounce it correctly, but do it anyway!

wrong:   *AIR*
right:     *UR* (rhymes with *fur*)

### 2.6.10 *espresso*

*Espresso* comes from the Italian word for *press*. It has nothing to do with the English word *express*.

wrong:   *eks•PRESS•o*
right:     *es•PRESS•o*

### 2.6.11 *February*

WARNING!!! Mispronouncing *February* is a sure way to get laughed at by the Grammar Police. In case you haven't noticed, there's an *r* after the *b*.

wrong:   *FEB•u•ar•y*
right:     *FEB•ru•ar•y*

### 2.6.12 *forbade*

The past form of *forbid* is pronounced wrong more often than it's pronounced right. It's a little-known fact that the second syllable, *bade,* is properly pronounced *bad.* It does not rhyme with *made.*

wrong:   *for•BADE* (rhymes with *made*)
right:     *for•BAD*

### 2.6.13 *forte*

This is one of those words that is so commonly mispronounced that, if you were to pronounce it correctly, people would think you'd made a mistake. So what do you do? Say it right? Say it wrong? Avoid it altogether? One of life's difficult decisions.

wrong: *for•TAY*
right: *FORT*

### 2.6.14 *Illinois*

WARNING!!! My home state is the most mispronounced state in the Union. Yes, there's an *s* on the end, but the name came from French explorers, and for that reason, the final consonant, *s,* is silent, as is common in French. Pronouncing the *s* can make you sound like a bumpkin, so don't.

wrong: *Ill•i•NOYZ*
right: *Ill•i•NOY*

### 2.6.15 *Javier*

Many English speakers who have studied French vaguely recall that the *ier* ending that many French words have is pronounced *eeAY* (the *r* being silent), so they apply this pronunciation rule to the name *Javier.* There's only one problem with that—*Javier* is a Spanish name, not a French name. The *r* is not silent.

wrong: *ha•vee•AY*
right: *ha•vee•AIR*

### 2.6.16 *library*

WARNING!!! Mispronouncing *library* is something the Grammar Police notice a mile away, so make sure you don't.

wrong: *LI•bar•y*
right: *LI•brar•y*

### 2.6.17 *mischievous*

WARNING!!! Mispronouncing *mischievous* can make you sound like a bumpkin. There are three syllables, not four.

wrong: *mis•CHEE•vee•us*
right: *MIS•chu•vus*

### 2.6.18 *picture*

WARNING!!! Mispronouncing *picture* is a sure way to sound like a bumpkin, so make sure you pronounce the *c.*

wrong: *PICH•er*
right: *PIK•chure*

### 2.6.19 *probably*

You *probly* say *probly.* Most people do, even some members of the Grammar Police (egad!), but when you want to use the very best English, say it right.

BREAK THE LANGUAGE BARRIER!

wrong:    *PROB•ly*
right:     *PRO•bab•ly*

## 2.6.20 *quay*

As we all know, a *quay* is like a wharf. Despite its weird spelling, it's properly pronounced *kee*.

wrong:    *KAY*
right:     *KEE*

## 2.6.21 *remunerate*

wrong:    *re•NU•mer•ate*
right:     *re•MEW•ner•ate*

## 2.6.22 *reprise*

wrong:    *re•PRIZE*
right:     *re•PREEZ*

## 2.6.23 *row*

No, not *row,* as in row your boat or sit in the first row. *Row* is a British term which means *argument.* It rhymes with *cow.* Amaze your British friends by getting it right.

wrong:    *ROO* (rhymes with *go*)
right:     *ROW* (rhymes with *cow*)

## 2.6.24 *sherbet*

wrong:    *SHER•bert*
right:     *SHER•bet*

## 2.6.25 *shire*

Another good way to astonish your British friends is by pronouncing this correctly. When the word *shire* stands alone, it rhymes with *fire,* but when it's stuck on the end of an English county, like Buckinghamshire or Lincolnshire, it's reduced to *shur* (rhymes with *fur*). Getting this wrong sounds dumb to the British, and you certainly don't want that, do you?

wrong:    *BUCK•ing•ham•shire,* etc. (*shire* rhymes with *fire*)
right:     *BUCK•ing•ham•shur,* etc. (*shire* rhymes with *fur*)

## 2.6.26 *via*

wrong:    *VY•a*
right:     *VEE•a*

## 2.6.27 *Xavier*

Pity the poor fellow named *Xavier* who has to endure a lifetime of having his name mispronounced. There is no *x* in Xavier. Yes, I know you see one, but it's pronounced as a *z.* Trust me. No matter how many sports announcers say *St. Ekzavier,* it's wrong.

Getting this right is a good way to impress the Grammar Police. Getting it wrong is a good way to sound dumb.

wrong:  *ek•ZA•vi•er*
right:   *ZA•vi•er*

**P**unctuation mistakes are something the Grammar Police notice. In fact, some mistakes are so common and considered so dumb by the Grammar Police that some mean-spirited members of the force have actually created websites of particularly dumb and funny examples. Do you want to end up on one of those sites? No, you don't, so keep reading.

# 3.1 · Problems with Commas

### 3.1.1 Comma splices—connecting sentences

Do these look OK to you?

> *Larry doesn't live in Los Angeles anymore, he moved to San Francisco last year.*
> *I wasn't angry with my son, I was disappointed.*
> *I'm pretty sure I failed the math test I had today, it was really hard.*
> *She sold her pickup truck, she bought an SUV.*
> *We shot at the same time. He missed, I didn't.*
> *She was really sick, she went to the doctor.*
> *I went shopping with my wife, I wanted to stay home and watch the game.*

If they do, then you're probably making the same mistake, known as a *comma splice*. A comma splice is two *independent clauses* incorrectly connected with a comma. What's an independent clause? Easy. An independent clause is simply a complete sentence—something that would make sense if it were alone and not connected to anything else. Sometimes two (or more) independent clause can be connected to make one longer sentence (known as a complex sentence). Doing it with a comma, however, isn't the right way to do it.

But sometimes the solution is not to connect them at all but rather to leave them as two sentences. For example,

> wrong: *Larry doesn't live in Los Angeles anymore, he moved to San Francisco last year.*
> right: *Larry doesn't live in Los Angeles anymore. He moved to San Francisco last year.*

> wrong: *I'm pretty sure I failed the math test I had today, it was really hard.*
> right: *I'm pretty sure I failed the math test I had today. It was really hard.*

Sometimes the solution is to connect them with a *conjunction*. Conjunctions (or more accurately *coordinating conjunctions*), are the words *and, but, for, nor, or, so* and *yet*. Which one you use depends on the relationship you want to show between the independent clauses. The most common are *and, but, or* and *so*. We can fix three of our examples with conjunctions.

> wrong: *I wasn't angry with my son, I was disappointed.*
> right: *I wasn't angry with my son, but I was disappointed.*

| wrong: | *She sold her pickup truck, she bought an SUV.* |
|--------|------------------------------------------------|
| right: | *She sold her pickup truck, and she bought an SUV.* |

| wrong: | *She was really sick, she went to the doctor.* |
|--------|------------------------------------------------|
| right: | *She was really sick, so she went to the doctor.* |

Notice that there are still commas in these sentences. They're not only permissible but required before a conjunction connecting independent clauses.

Sometimes the best solution is to simply rewrite the sentence, saying the same thing in a different way.

| wrong: | *She was really sick, she went to the doctor.* |
|--------|------------------------------------------------|
| right: | *Because she was really sick, she went to the doctor.* |
| right: | *She went to the doctor because she was really sick.* |

| wrong: | *I went shopping with my wife, I wanted to stay home and watch the game.* |
|--------|------------------------------------------------|
| right: | *Although I went shopping with my wife, I wanted to stay home and watch the game.* |
| right: | *I went shopping with my wife although I wanted to stay home and watch the game.* |

Notice that there are commas in these examples,

*Because she was really sick, she went to the doctor.*
*Although I went shopping with my wife, I wanted to stay home and watch the game.*

but no commas in these:

*She went to the doctor because she was really sick.*
*I went shopping with my wife although I wanted to stay home and watch the game.*

Why? That's because

*because she was really sick*

and

*although I wanted to stay home and watch the game*

are what are called *dependent clauses.* That means they do not make sense alone. When dependent clauses begin a sentence, a comma is required after the dependent clause. When it follows the independent clause, using a comma is incorrect. Be careful about that. Using a comma in sentences with *because* is a common mistake.

| wrong: | *I went to the doctor, because I was really sick.* |
|--------|------------------------------------------------|
| right: | *I went to the doctor because I was really sick.* |

And finally, another way to fix a comma splice is with a *semicolon,* but this is generally not the best solution. Semicolons have their uses, but careful writers are very sparing in their use. Short and similarly constructed sentences can be connected with semicolons.

| wrong: | *We shot at the same time. He missed, I didn't.* |
|--------|------------------------------------------------|
| right: | *We shot at the same time. He missed; I didn't.* |

There is very rarely a time when a semicolon is the only solution, so if you're not sure about the right way to use a semicolon, it's best to leave it to the professionals.

## 3.1.2 When using a comma is wrong

Do these look OK to you?

*Larry took a shower, and went to bed.*
*Sofia studied like crazy for the test, but failed it anyway.*

Do these seem like what we just talked about—two independent clauses joined with a conjunction and therefore requiring a comma? If they do, look again. Using commas in sentences like these is a common mistake.

Remember that a comma is used to join two independent clauses, and that the test to see if a clause is independent is that it makes sense alone. Do these make sense alone?

*Went to bed.*
*Failed it anyway.*

No, they don't. They don't have a subject. Why not? Because when the subject of both clauses is the same, it's optional whether the subject is repeated or omitted. When it is omitted, the result is not two independent clauses joined with a conjunction but one independent clause with two verbs.

two independent clauses—comma required: *He took a shower, and he went to bed.*
omitted second subject—no comma required: *He took a shower and went to bed.*

two independent clauses—comma required: *Sofia studied like crazy for the test, but she failed it anyway.*
omitted second subject—no comma required: *Sofia studied like crazy for the test but failed it anyway.*

Does this look OK to you?

*I went to the doctor, because I was sick.*

This is another common mistake. No comma is required when the independent clause precedes the dependent clause.

wrong: *Linda refused to marry me, because my English grammar was so bad.*
right: *Linda refused to marry me because my English grammar was so bad.*

Do these look OK to you?

*She wants to study engineering, or law.*
*Last year I went to France, and Spain.*

We saw that commas are required in a series of three or more, but no comma is required when there are only two.

wrong: *She wants to study engineering, or law.*
right: *She wants to study engineering or law.*

wrong: *Last year I went to France, and Spain.*
right: *Last year I went to France and Spain.*

## Quiz 3.1.1-3.1.2
Each of these sentences has an error. Find it and correct it.

1. I need to see the doctor, this pain is killing me.

2. I haven't seen that movie, I heard it was really good.

3. Carlos went on a diet, he lost 25 lbs.

4. We were really tired, we went to bed.

5. We canceled the picnic, because it was cold and rainy.

6. My sister went to a fertility specialist, and ended up having triplets.

7. The movie got great reviews, but was a huge flop.

### 3.1.3 When commas are optional
Members and wannabe members of the Grammar Police, leading pathetic, empty lives with little to do other than nitpick about other people's English, have spent countless hours raging over one of the great punctuation debates of our time—the *serial comma,* also known as the *Oxford comma.*

One use of commas is to separate items in a series. A series is three or more like items in a clause separated by commas. They can be nouns, verbs, adjectives, adverbs and a variety of other grammatical structures—even independent clauses. As we saw in 1.7.1, they need to be parallel, in other words, all in the same form.

Normally *and* or *or* appears before the final element in the series. So what's the big deal? It's whether a comma should be used after the second to last item (and therefore before the conjunction).

For example, notice the comma after *apples* in the first example.

> with serial comma:      *I bought potatoes, onions, bananas, apples, and oranges.*
> without a serial comma:  *I bought potatoes, onions, bananas, apples and oranges.*

Yep, that's what it's all about. I won't bore you with all the arguments for and against the use of serial commas. The debate rages on without a winner, so neither school of thought can be considered incorrect. I personally do not use serial commas, but using them is not universally condemned by the Grammar Police. The main thing is to be consistent. When proper punctuation matters, either never use serial commas or always use them.

## 3.2 • Problems with Apostrophes
WARNING!!! This is another area where many people make mistakes. So common and often so dumb are these mistakes that there are several websites in which snide, heartless members of the Grammar Police contribute examples for other members to laugh at. Cruel, isn't it? Do you want people snickering at you behind your back when they read something you've written? Of course not, so read on.

BREAK THE LANGUAGE BARRIER!

Apostrophes have two unproblematic functions in English and, some people mistakenly believe, other functions.

## 3.2.1 Contractions

Few people get this wrong. We can combine two words to make one with an apostrophe: *do + not = don't, I + have = I've*. No need to go into this further. The only slight complication is that *can't* starts out as *cannot*, which isn't two words but one. Writing *cannot* as *can not* is a common mistake.

## 3.2.2 Possessive nouns

The idea of possession, that something belongs to something or someone else, can be shown with apostrophes. When the noun is singular, this is done with *'s*.

> *David's shoes are dirty.*
> *I washed my son's clothes but not my daughter's.*

When singular nouns end with *s*, we normally add *'s*.

> *I went to my boss's office.*
> *One of the bus's wheels fell off before the plunge.*

But what about names? Not everyone agrees. Some say that *'s* should always be added.

> *Do you know what Marcos's telephone number is?*
> *Carlos's grades are always excellent.*

But others maintain, for no good reason that I can figure out, that Biblical and classical names should be treated differently—that only an apostrophe should be added.

> *Zeus was Hercules' father.*
> *Most people celebrate Jesus' birthday on December 25.*

This is considered sort of old fashioned by some members of the Grammar Police, and the trend is to use *'s* with all names, Biblical, classical or otherwise.

When a noun is plural, we normally add *s'*.

> *The teacher was shocked at how bad her students' grades were.*
> *I have three cars, and all of my cars' brakes are bad.*

However, when the noun is an irregular plural which does not end with *s*, like *men, women, children,* or *people*, we add *'s*.

> *I met with my children's teacher.*
> *My 12-year-old son is so tall that he has to buy his clothes in the men's department.*

## 3.2.3 Problematic—*it's* or *its*?

WARNING!!! We have seen that we make possessive nouns with *'s*, but don't do it with the possessive adjective *its*. *It's* is a contraction of *it is* or *it has*—an apostrophe is correct in this case. But no apostrophe belongs in the possessive adjective *its*. (The other possessive adjectives are *my, your, his, her, our, your* and *their*.) This mistake is very common and one we members of the Grammar Police can spot a mile away. So watch it!

wrong and dumb:     *You can't judge a book by it's cover.*
right and not dumb:     *You can't judge a book by its cover.*

## 3.2.4 Problematic—plural nouns

WARNING!!! By far, the number one mistake people make with apostrophes is using them in plurals. Apostrophes DO NOT belong in plurals. Writing, for example, *book's* when you mean *books, car's* when you mean *cars, dog's* when you mean *dogs,* is totally wrong and totally dumb, so don't do it!

wrong and dumb:     *Yesterday, I bought banana's, orange's and apple's.*
right and not dumb:     *Yesterday, I bought bananas, oranges and apples.*

## 3.2.5 Problematic—plurals of names

Do not use apostrophes with plural names.

wrong:     *There are three Jennifer's in my son's class.*
right:     *There are three Jennifers in my son's class.*

If the name ends with *y,* do not change it to *ie.*

wrong:     *There are two Sallies in my son's class.*
right:     *There are two Sallys in my son's class.*

## 3.2.6 Problematic—plurals of numerals

A common mistake is using apostrophes with numerals. There's just no reason for it.

wrong:     *There are three 6's in my telephone number.*
right:     *There are three 6s in my telephone number.*

wrong:     *It's going to be in the 90's tomorrow.*
right:     *It's going to be in the 90s tomorrow.*

wrong:     *CDs became popular in the 1980's.*
right:     *CDs became popular in the 1980s.*

wrong:     *Cars in the 60's and 70's were bigger than they are today.*
right:     *Cars in the 60s and 70s were bigger than they are today.*

Regarding plurals of decades, like the examples above, using only *s* (like *60s* and *70s*) is acceptable, but if you want to be extra precise about punctuation, you can use an apostrophe before the first numeral.

*Cars in the '60s and '70s were bigger than they are today.*

Why? It relates to the function of an apostrophe in a contraction. The apostrophe takes the place of something that has been omitted. In this case it's *19* that has been omitted. But to do this correctly, the apostrophe must be like this (look carefully): ' and not like this: '. If you type an apostrophe followed by a numeral or letter, Microsoft Word will instead give you an inverted quotation mark. To force an apostrophe out of Word, type any numeral or letter, then the apostrophe and then the numeral or letter you want to follow the apostrophe. After that, delete the numeral or letter before the apostrophe. Voilà!

### 3.2.7 Problematic—plurals of abbreviations

Be careful here. This mistake can make you look dumb. There is no reason for apostrophes with plural abbreviations.

wrong and dumb: *I have two BA's and an MA.*
right and not dumb: *I have two BAs and an MA.*

wrong and dumb: *The pilot saw three UFO's.*
right and not dumb: *The pilot saw three UFOs.*

wrong and dumb: *I bought two DVD's yesterday.*
right and not dumb: *I bought two DVDs yesterday.*

### Quiz 3.2.3-3.2.7

Each of these sentences has one or more errors. Find them and correct them.

1. The airplane crashed, because one of it's engine's fell off.

2. Its surprising that it's roof wasn't torn off by the tornado.

3. My sister's kid's rode their bike's to the ice cream shop, but it's door's were locked.

4. In Britain, there were four King George's.

5. The 60's was a tumultuous decade in USA.

6. Yesterday the temperature got down to the low 20's.

7. After three DUI's, he was sentenced to a year in jail.

### 3.2.8 Problematic—plurals of letters

When words, numbers and letters are discussed as words, letters and numbers, many people feel compelled to add an apostrophe. There is some disagreement among Grammar Police members because there is, admittedly, some logic to using an apostrophe in cases such as these. Sometimes it helps to prevent a misreading of what has been written. For example,

*The name Aaron starts with two* a*'s.*

That's pretty clear, I think, but would it be equally clear without the apostrophe or italics, as it would normally be written (demonstrated below)?

The name Aaron starts with two as.

I don't think so. In this sentence, I reluctantly admit, a good case could be made for using an apostrophe that deviates from the rules of punctuation. Personally, it troubles me to use erroneous apostrophes, but I admit that they sometimes serve a purpose. My advice is to avoid this if possible, but if there is a serious danger of confusion, go for it.

### 3.2.9 Problematic—plurals of words discussed as words

Here is our other problematic use of apostrophes—when words are discussed as words. Again, members of the Grammar Police can't come to an agreement about this. Some think it's perfectly acceptable; some hate it. I tend to hate it, but I do see an occasional need for it. Why is it problematic? Because, as with plurals of letters, a case can be made for violating punctuation rules to avoid confusion.

The example below is pretty easy to figure out without apostrophes.

*That's final! No ifs, ands or buts.*

But what about these?

*There were three nos for every yes.*
*A list of dos and don'ts.*

A reader could easily stumble over *nos* and *dos,* and I reluctantly admit that an apostrophe (*no's* and *do's*) would prevent that. So once again, my advice is to avoid apostrophes with plurals of words discussed as words if possible, but if there is a serious danger of confusion, be a rebel and go for it.

## 3.3 • Other Punctuation Problems

### 3.3.1 Problems with quotation marks

WARNING!!! This is another area where many people make mistakes, much to the amusement of some cruel-hearted members of the Grammar Police who post examples of these mistakes on the Internet. Just do a Google search on "unnecessary quotation marks" and you'll see what I mean.

And it's really very easy. Quotation marks are used for—brace yourself—quotations. They are not used for emphasis. Here are some examples of totally dumb quotation marks that I've adapted from examples on some of the websites I mentioned.

*Check out our "new" selection of cheeses.*
*"Gluten Free" section*
*Absolutely "NO" Dogs in the Restroom*
*"Coldest" Beer in Town*
*No Customers "Allowed" Beyond This Point*
*"Fresh" Seafood*
*The picnic has been "canceled"*
*Please stay behind the white line when alarm is "ringing"*
*"Sorry" Cash Only Today. Credit Card Machine is "Broken"*
*All "Cereals" 2 for $6.00*
*"Do Not" Throw Away When Empty*
*Lunch is "served" "Dig" in*
*We sincerely "Thank You" for recommending us*
*Lobby "Closed"*

I could go on—there are many more—but I'm starting to feel sick to my stomach. The point is that all of the quotation marks above are totally unnecessary, totally wrong and totally dumb. Don't be dumb—use quotation marks only for quotations.

## Quiz 3.3.1

Each of these sentences has an error. Find it and correct it.

1. Please turn handle "slowly"

2. Snack Bar Will Be "Closed" Today

3. Employees Must "Wash Hands"

4. Do "Not" Block This Way

5. "Temporarily" Out of Service

6. Restrooms "Across the Street"

## 3.3.2 Problems with hyphens

People tend to overuse hyphens. Hyphens have their place, but they frequently appear where they don't belong.

One area of confusion is when they're used in *compound adjectives*. A compound adjective is two or more words that are not adjectives (or at least one of them isn't) stuck together with hyphens and used as an adjective. All sorts of things can be used to make compound adjectives—nouns, past participles, present participles (verbs with *ing* on the end), adverbs, numbers, periods of time, amounts of money. For example,

*a $400-a-night hotel room*
*a 50-minute class*
*a bitter-sweet memory*
*a do-it-yourself-project*
*a full-time job*
*a gas-powered engine*
*a labor-saving device*
*a long-lasting relationship*
*a well-known author*
*an old-fashioned idea*

Here's the important idea—it's only a compound adjective when it precedes the noun. After the noun, it isn't a compound adjective, so no hyphens are required. That's the mistake many people make.

before the noun—hyphen required:    *He has a full-time job.*
after the noun—no hyphen required:    *His job is full time.*

before the noun—hyphen required:    *I have a 16-year-old daughter.*
after the noun—no hyphen required:    *My daughter is 16 years old.*

before the noun—hyphen required:    *I stayed in a $400-a-night hotel room.* (Say *dollar,* not *dollars.*)
after the noun—no hyphen required:    *My hotel room cost $400 a night.* (Say *dollars,* not *dollar.*)

Speaking of compound adjectives, another common mistake is making them plural. You can say that you bought *20 feet of rope* but not that you bought a *20-feet rope.*

wrong:   *I bought a 20-feet rope.*
wrong:   *I bought 20 foot of rope.*
right:    *I bought a 20-foot rope.*
right:    *I bought 20 feet of rope.*
right:    *The rope I bought is 20 feet long.*

Many use unnecessary hyphens when attaching *prefixes* and *suffixes* (extra bits attached to the beginning or end of a word).

Here are some examples of unnecessary hyphens.

wrong:   *anti-communist*
right:    *anticommunist*

wrong:   *bi-coastal*
right:    *bicoastal*

wrong:   *child-like*
right:    *childlike*

wrong:   *mid-field*
right:    *midfield*

wrong:   *nation-wide*
right:    *nationwide*

wrong:   *non-stick*
right:    *nonstick*

wrong:   *over-cook*
right:    *overcook*

wrong:   *post-war*
right:    *postwar*

wrong:   *romance-wise*
right:    *romancewise* (As in *My life is a total disaster romancewise.*)

wrong:   *semi-truck*
right:    *semitruck*

wrong:   *sub-human*
right:    *subhuman*

However, there are some exceptions.

When a word begins with a capital letter, a hyphen is used.

*anti-American*
*trans-Atlantic*

When there's a danger of a word being misunderstood as another word, a hyphen is permissible. For example, *re-cover* (cover again), *re-sign* (sign again), *re-sent* (sent again), *re-sort* (sort again), *re-lease* (lease again). Without hyphens, these words could easily be misread as *recover, resign, resort* and *release,* all of which have different meanings.

Also, when people might stumble over the pronunciation of a word because of a double vowel, a hyphen can prevent this. For example,

*co-opt*
*de-emphasize*

## Quiz 3.3.2
Some of these sentences have an error. Find them and correct them.

1. We have a 17 year old daughter.

2. Our son is 21 years old.

3. Do you work full time?

4. Yes, I have a full time job.

5. Our house has five bedrooms.

6. We live in a five bedroom house.

7. I have a 35 foot boat.

### 3.3.3 Problems with title capitalization
Many people mistakenly capitalize every word in a title, however articles (*a, an* and *the*), coordinating conjunctions (*and, but, for, nor, or, so* and *yet*) and prepositions (for example, *in, on, at, of, with, by under, next to*) should not be capitalized unless they are the first word in a title—the first word should always be capitalized. There are style manuals with slight variations on these rules, but generally speaking, this is what it boils down to. For example,

*To Kill a Mocking Bird*
*The Lord of the Rings*
*Gone with the Wind*
*Harry Potter and the Sorcerer's Stone*

## Quiz 3.3.3
Circle the letters which should be capitalized.

1. and then there were none

2. midnight in the garden of good and evil

3. so long, and thanks for all the fish

4. the hitchhiker's guide to the galaxy

### 3.3.4 Italics or quotation marks with titles?

Members of the Grammar Police, naturally, argue over the finer points here, but generally speaking, longer works, like books, films, CDs and names of newspapers or magazines should be italicized, but shorter pieces which might be discussed as being included in a longer work like a song on a CD or album, an article in a newspaper or magazine or a chapter in a book, should be in quotation marks (as they are properly called—not *quotes*!) For example,

| | |
|---|---|
| film: | Have you ever seen *Citizen Kane*? |
| song: | My favorite Moody Blues song is "Candle of Life" on *To Our Children's Children's Children*. |
| book: | "The Quidditch World Cup" is the eighth chapter in *Harry Potter and the Goblet of Fire*. |
| magazine: | I wrote an article titled "New World Vikings" for *World Explorer*. |
| newspaper: | Did you read the article "The Myth of the American Dream" in the *New York Times*? |

A few other points. Back in ancient times, when people used typewriters, on which italicizing was impossible, the rule about italicizing longer works used to be to underline them. That's very old fashioned, so don't do it. Also, members of the Grammar Police can't agree whether *the* should be capitalized when it's part of the name of a newspaper of magazine. ( *I read the New York Times* or *I read The New York Times*?) Either way is acceptable, but be consistent.

## Quiz 3.3.4

Circle the titles that should be in italics and underline those that should be in quotation marks.

1. I watched Butch Cassidy and the Sundance Kid last night. It was a great movie.

2. Billie Jean was a song on Michael Jackson's album Thriller.

3. Gentlemen of New South Wales is the title of the tenth chapter of Fatal Shore.

4. I'm reading an article named Lost Tombs of the Pharaohs in a magazine called History Revealed.

5. There was an article titled The Fury of Forgotten Voters in today's Daily Mail newspaper.

### 3.3.5 *resume, resumé* or *résumé?*

This word, borrowed from French, is acceptable either with accents on both *e*s or neither. *Resume* is most common in US English and perfectly fine, but if you want to show off, use two accents, not one (*résumé*).

**1 / Quiz 1.1.1 & 1.1.2**
1. They are in the garage.
2. My sister is crazy.
3. She is really angry.
4. Tom and Bob are at the beach.
5. Her husband is a pilot.

**2 / Quiz 1.1.3**
1. They were going to the mall.
2. Mary and I were really tired after working all day.
3. Were you at the party last night?
4. When were you at the mall?
5. The students weren't listening to the teacher.

**3 / Quiz 1.1.4**
1. If she were the boss, what do you think she would change around here?
2. I wouldn't do that if I were you.
3. What would you tell him if he were here?
4. If I weren't a teacher, I'd like to be a scientist.
5. I'd give you a ride if my car weren't in the shop.

**3 / Quiz 1.1.5 & 1.1.6**
1. I wish my son weren't so lazy.
2. Why do you talk to me as if I were an idiot?
3. Don't you wish today were Friday?
4. My husband acts as though I were invisible.
5. I think he wishes he were single

**6 / Quiz 1.2.1**
1. She and I went to the mall.
2. She and her sister speak French.
3. My father is going with my sister and me.
4. Sofia, Rosa, Carlos and I went to a Mexican restaurant.
5. Let's keep this between you and me.

**7 / Quiz 1.2.2**
1. Nobody sings better than she.
   Nobody sings better than she does.
2. Do you think Carlos is taller than I?
   Do you think Carlos is taller than I am?
3. I don't know how anyone could be stupider than he.
   I don't know how anyone could be stupider than he is.
4. We have more experience than they.
   We have more experience than they do.
5. I don't think anyone deserves this award more than we.
   I don't think anyone deserves this award more than we do.

**9 / Quiz 1.2.4**
1. John and I worked on the project together.

2. After the class, I need to talk to Sarah and you.
3. You may turn in your report to Prof. Davis or me.
4. Frank and I will contact either Maria or you after we arrive.
5. Do you want to come with Ali and me?

## 10 / Quiz 1.2.5

1. Who didn't finish her homework?
2. When someone calls in sick, he or she has to bring a doctor's note.
   When people call in sick, they have to bring a doctor's note.
3. If I knew who stole my bike, I'd punch him or her in the face.
4. If a student loses his or her ID, he or she has to talk to the principal.
   If students lose their IDs, they have to talk to the principal.
5. Each girl must complete the assignment herself. No one can help her.

## 12/ Quiz 1.2.7

1. It's a beautiful house, but its roof is in really bad condition.
2. The restaurant raised its prices.
3. It's well known that you can't judge a book by its cover.
4. Chicago is known for its skyline.
5. It's been a long time since its design was changed.

## 13 / Quiz 1.2.8

1. Who
2. whom
3. whomever
4. whom
5. who

## 14 / Quiz 1.2.9

1. These kinds of problems make me really angry.
2. Do you like those kinds of cookies?
3. I told my daughter to stay away from those types of guys.
4. He loves to read these sorts of books.
5. I don't like being around these kinds of dogs.

## 15 / Quiz 1.2.10

1. I'm sick and tired of your complaining!
2. I was really shocked at his having quit his job.
3. Mary's selling her house and moving to Alaska really surprised me.
4. My wife was furious about my losing the house in a poker game.
5. I hate my son's working as a lion tamer.

## 16 / Quiz 1.3.1

1. There are three reasons I don't want to do it.
2. David thinks there are aliens on the moon.
3. There are some people waiting to see you.
4. There are a lot of mice living in our kitchen.
5. Do you know if there are 30 days in June or 31?

## 18 / Quiz 1.3.2

1. The divers were eaten by a group of giant octopuses.
2. Both of my brothers-in-law speak Spanish.
3. There were four chiefs of staff during the Obama administration.
4. There were two attorneys general during the Obama administration.
5. This phenomenon cannot be explained.

## 19 / Quiz 1.3.3

1. Neither of those bookstores has the book I'm looking for.
2. Either of these routes is OK.
3. Neither of my kids wants to come for Christmas dinner.
4. Neither the chief of the police nor the detectives has a clue who did it.
5. If either of your brothers wants to come, it's OK with me.

## 20 / Quiz 1.3.4 & 1.3.5

1. Everybody that I talked to agrees with me.
2. Someone forgot his umbrella.
   Someone forgot his or her umbrella.
3. Each of my cats has different personalities.
4. Anyone who believes that is crazy.
5. Each of these pairs of shoes is the wrong size.

## 21 / Quiz 1.3.7

1. were
2. is
3. go
4. have
5. was

## 22 / Quiz 1.4.1

1. Doesn't she have beautiful eyes?
2. Jimmy doesn't like vegetables.
3. I want to go out, but my wife doesn't.
4. Why doesn't Carlos like Maria?
5. I think she doesn't love me anymore.

## 22 / Quiz 1.4.2

1. I didn't go anywhere yesterday.
2. She doesn't want anything to eat.
3. Mark doesn't trust anybody.
4. The doctor can't do anything for him.
5. Didn't you go anywhere last night?

## 23 / Quiz 1.5.1

1. If he had asked me, I would have told him.
2. I would have bought some beer if I had known David was coming.
3. Tom wishes he had finished high school.
4. If the Knicks had won, I would have made 50 bucks.
5. You wouldn't be so sick if you hadn't eaten like such a pig.

## 24 / Quiz 1.5.2

1. I'm really hungry. I haven't eaten all day.
2. Have you finished your homework yet?
3. We don't want to go there again. We've already gone there.
4. I told him to do it, but he still hasn't done it.
5. She keeps saying she's going to quit smoking, but she still hasn't.

## 24 / Quiz 1.5.3

Last week, my son graduated from high school. We attended his graduation and then went to a nice restaurant where we had a nice dinner, and we gave him a new watch as a graduation present. After that, we visited his grandparents. They wanted to go out to dinner, but we told them that we had already had dinner.

## 25 / Quiz 1.5.4

1. I'm sorry I missed Sarah. I would have liked to see her.
2. Why didn't you call me? I would have liked to go with you.
3. That's funny! I would like to have been there when it happened.
4. I had no idea. I would like to have been informed of this in advance.

## 27 / Quiz 1.6.1

1. Some of my students are awfully dumb.
2. OK
3. Michael drives terribly.
4. OK
5. These cookies came out perfectly.
6. Elaine dances awfully.
7. OK
8. My neighbors were arguing really loudly.
9. Thank you. That was really nice of you.
10. OK
11. Lisa is very sensitive, so treat her nicely.
12. OK
13. OK
14. Tom is really angry.
15. If you think that's a real diamond, you're really stupid.
16. OK
17. Hey! You'd better take me seriously. I'm not joking.
18. OK
19. David is working so slowly that I think he'll never finish this project.
20. We need to go directly to the airport. I don't have time to stop.
21. OK
22. That was excellent! You did it just beautifully.

## 28 / Quiz 1.6.2

1. OK
2. Fewer than 1,000 people live in my town.
3. OK
4. OK
5. I like shopping early in the morning because there are fewer people in the stores.

## 29 / Quiz 1.6.3

1. It was a perfect experience.
2. This is the most nearly perfect diet I ever tried.
3. The police went back and did a more nearly complete search of the suspect's house.
   The police went back and did a more thorough search of the suspect's house.
4. Venice is a unique city.
5. Her engagement ring is unique. I've never seen another one like it.

## 30 / Quiz 1.6.4

1. I feel bad about hurting her feelings.
2. My wife speaks Spanish really well.
3. Mark feels bad because he did badly on the test.
4. Jim plays basketball really badly.

## 31 / Quiz 1.6.5

1. I drank only one cup of coffee.

2. She wants only two children.
3. Carlos is going only to the reception and not the wedding.
4. I'm sorry. I said that only because I was angry.
5. You're allowed only three sick days a year.

### 33 / Quiz 1.7.1
1. Every evening, I make dinner, wash the dishes and do my homework.
2. My brother likes to swim, to play football and to go fishing.
   My brother likes to swim, play football and go fishing.
3. I hate waking up early and working in the hot sun all day.
   I hate to wake up early and to work in the hot sun all day.
   I hate to wake up early and work in the hot sun all day.
4. The boss likes me because I'm always on time, I do my work well and I never complain.
5. To succeed in college, you must do the following: study hard, attend every class and take notes.

### 33 / Quiz 1.7.2
1. My landlord requires a month's notice before ending the rental agreement.
2. I bought twenty dollars' worth of gas.
3. In ten days' time I'll be in Cancun.
4. He'll be out of jail in three years' time.
5. My stupid husband lost two months' salary in Las Vegas.

### 34 / Quiz 1.7.3
1. Do you have to work on Saturday?
   Have you got to work on Saturday?
2. I don't have a car.
   I haven't got a car.
3. They don't have to hand in their homework till next week.
   They haven't got to hand in their homework till next week.
4. What do we have to do tomorrow?
   What have we got to do tomorrow?
5. She doesn't have a penny to her name.
   She hasn't got a penny to her name.

### 36 / Quiz 1.7.4
1. Phew, that meteor missed me by just a few inches. If it had hit me, I might have been killed.
2. OK
3. Jim told me he might have gotten lost on the way here if it weren't for his GPS.
4. The policeman told me he might have been killed if he hadn't been wearing a bulletproof vest.
5. OK

### 36 / Quiz 1.7.5-1.7.8
1. Where's my cell phone?
2. I have no idea where it it.
3. I'm going to try to get my boss to give me Friday off.
4. My father told me to be sure to lock the door when I leave.
5. Why do I want to quit my job? The reason is that the pay is so low.

### 37 / Quiz 1.7.9-1.7.10
1. The construction guys didn't build the deck as I asked them to.
2. My father would never eat food such as clams or oysters.
3. On a low carb diet you need to avoid foods such as bread, rice and pasta.

4. He screwed it up just as I knew he would.

5. I would never want to live in a hot, humid city such as Houston or New Orleans.

## 37 / Quiz 1.7.11

1. Where did you use to work?

2. Didn't you use to be a lot thinner?

3. My father used to have truck.

4. Did he use to live in Alaska?

5. I always used to think he was an idiot, and I was right.

## 38 / Quiz 1.7.12

1. Not a single student in any of the math classes has a chance of passing the test.

2. Sean is one of my cousins who live in France.

3. One of the people that were at the party was kind of weird.

4. One of the things that bother me about him is how much he drinks

5. Dr. Smith is one of the few people who understand quantum physics.

## 39 / Quiz 1.7.13-1.7.14 [possible answers]

1. The doctor prescribed antibiotics.

   The doctor prescribed antibiotics and other things.

2. When he told me he wanted to quit his job and join the circus, I said no way!

## 41 / Quiz 1.8.1-1.8.5

Tricked you. There's nothing wrong with any of these sentences.

## 49 / Quiz 2.1.1-2.1.26

1. If you're traveling in Switzerland, be sure to take a lot of money.

2. Oh, I see. That's a another thing. [one possible answer]

3. In school today we studied the abolition of slavery.

4. Sorry to burst your balloon, Lisa, but he's lying to you.

5. My mother didn't think it was funny when I compared her corned beef hash to dog food.

6. I compared my plan with his, and mine is better in every way.

7. New York City comprises five boroughs.

8. The new king will be crowned next week.

9. The terrorist cell was wiped out. There wasn't a single survivor. [one possible answer]

10. How is American English different from British English?

11. I need to buy 20-foot of rope.

12. Captain Kidd was hanged in 1701.

13. My father had a lot of old fashioned ideas.

14. The shoe store is between the book store and the supermarket.

15. The cannibals dropped the missionary into a cauldron of boiling water.

16. When my mother didn't answer the door, I had to break in to see if she was OK.

17. I'm going to buy a Ferrari regardless of what my wife says.

18. I've told you a billion times. The answer is no.

19. These mementos bring back a lot of memories.

20. Carlos rescued a man who fell onto the subway tracks.

21. I turned the TV on to watch the game.

22. My wife bought two pairs of shoes and three pairs of pants.

23. I wonder what percentage of people are left-handed.

24. It's quite a way from here to there.

25. Anyway, all I called about was to ask you if you want to go anywhere tomorrow, so if you do, let me know.

1. There was a gas leak, and the house blew up.
2. I can't use my printer. It's broken.
3. He came here last week, but I didn't see him.
4. He has come here many times.
5. The police think David may have done it.
6. I dragged his body to the river and threw him in.
7. Lisa's boyfriend has drunk all her beer.
8. Have you ever gone to Disney World?
9. I was sick yesterday, so I just lay in bed and watched TV.
10. Have you just been lying there all day?
11. You've lain there all day watching TV. Get up, you bum!
12. I've never ridden a motorcycle.
13. I haven't run so fast since the last time Godzilla attacked.
14. The boat sank after it sprang a leak.
15. I've seen it with my own eyes.
16. We were all shaken by the news.
17. The class was so boring that I sneaked out of the classroom.
18. He was all torn up when he learned of the tragedy.
19. My mother threw out all my baseball cards.
20. He's written to her many times, but she never answers.

1. Our hospital has the most advanced medical technology.
2. Some believe that the US had advance knowledge of the Pearl Harbor attack.
3. Lisa's shy and averse to being the center of attention.
4. My application got lost among the other 20 applications.
5. What number of guests are coming to your wedding?
6. We're really eager to go on vacation next month.
7. The caller asked for Bob, but I didn't know if he was referring to Bob Jr. or Bob Sr.
8. The boss asked me to apprise him of the problems at the Nashville office.
9. Larry's flight to Chicago left six hours ago. Since it's a three-hour flight, I assume he's in Chicago now.
10. We got cheated at a bazaar in Istanbul.
11. This doesn't make any sense at all. It's really bizarre.
12. I was not amused by his stupid jokes.
13. I have no family besides my sister.
14. The explorers left a cache of food for the return journey.
15. People pay high prices for Rolex watches mainly because the name has a certain cachet.
16. The capital of Illinois is Springfield.
17. The state's capitol building was completed in 1868.
18. In many countries, the government censors the Internet.
19. The senator was censured for his racist comments.
20. Yesterday, my teacher complimented me on how good my report was.
21. The woman at the cosmetics counter said this shade of lip stick would complement my eye color.
22. The factory operates 24/7. Production is continuous.
23. I didn't want to go to the ballet, but my wife persuaded me to go.
24. Members of the council voted in favor of the agreement.
25. My parents counseled me not to major in philosophy, but I didn't listen.

26. There was a long queue at the British Museum.
27. When David passed out face first into a plate of spaghetti, that was my cue to close the bar.
28. The Internet and TV are no longer bundled. Now they are discrete services.
29. Don't tell my sister anything. She's incapable of being discreet.
30. Lisa thinks I'm boring. She's uninterested in anything I say.
31. When I moved to Alaska from Rhode Island, I was amazed at the enormousness of the state.
32. When my parents were killed, I was overwhelmed by the enormity of my loss.
33. Margaret Mitchell's only book was titled *Gone with the Wind.*
34. Just leave well enough alone. If you do anything, it will just exacerbate the situation.
35. The further I investigate this matter, the more shocked I become.
36. My daughter has a flair for music.
37. They thought the forest fire was out, but then it flared up again.
38. Did you see how Mary was flaunting her new engagement ring at work today?
39. Many young people flout society's conventions.
40. I asked Professor Davis to write a foreword for my book.
41. It was a grisly crime scene.
42. Sadly, David learned that grizzly bears aren't as cuddly as he thought.
43. After I adopted a healthful diet, I lost weight and felt a lot better.
44. My sister isn't healthy. She's in the hospital again.
45. The missile homed in on the target and totally destroyed it.
46. I was sure the pink elephant was real, but it was only an alcohol-induced delusion.
47. What was your sister implying when she commented that I used to be so thin?
48. When the HR guy suggested I update my résumé, I inferred that I was going to be laid off soon.
49. It really irritates me when you never let me finish a sentence.
50. My brother-in-law asked me to lend him my lawn mower.
51. I absolutely loathe public speaking.
52. After what happened last time, my sister is loath to ever invite her mother-in-law to another dinner party.
53. One of my students has several screws loose.
54. If we lose this game, we have no chance of making it to the finals.
55. I felt nauseated when I saw the crime scene photos.
56. The doctor was famous for treating poor people at no charge.
57. Carlos wasn't in the least bit fazed by the enormous challenge he faced.
58. It's past 8:00, so that means we're late for work.
59. Larry passed the ball to Carlos.
60. I took a peek at my brother's photos of mountain peaks, and it piqued my interest in mountain climbing.
61. The pathetic member of the Grammar Police pores over grammar books all day long.
62. Your doctor may prescribe creams and ointments that you should use for your psoriasis.
63. There are laws which proscribe discrimination based on race and gender.
64. The principal wants me to come to his office after class.
65. Separation of powers is a fundamental principle of American democracy.
66. One of my favorite quotations is "If you want to make God laugh, tell him about your plans."
67. I gave the interior decorator free rein to do anything she wanted.
68. Edward VI reigned for only six years.
69. The company created a new web site.
70. The developers chose a site for the new mall.
71. At the meeting, the CEO cited poor customer service as the main reason that revenue had

dropped in recent years.
72. When I cut off my toe while chopping wood, it took forever to stanch the bleeding.
73. I exercise on a stationary bicycle.
74. We went to a stationery store to buy some paper and pens.
75. Their car is over there, next to mine.
76. I don't want to go outside. It's too hot.
77. Do you know whether or not the weather guy is forecasting rain?
78. The man whose car was stolen had to take the bus to work.
79. Do you know who's going to the meeting?
80. You're really starting to make me angry!

## 72 / Quiz 2.4.1-2.4.10
1. Mary lost a lot of money in Las Vegas.
2. I've already seen that movie. I don't want to see it again.
3. I'm all ready for my vacation.
4. There are no problems. Everything is all right.
5. Altogether, there were 42 people on the bus when it plunged into the gorge.
6. The boss wants the employees all together to hear the announcement.
7. She's not married anymore.
8. I'm all out of money. I don't have any more.
9. I don't like any one of my wife's relatives.
10. Did anyone call while I was away?
11. I'm really tired. I need to rest awhile.
12. It's been a while since I last saw her.
13. Mass shootings are an everyday event in the USA.
14. I drink coffee every day.
15. I couldn't believe it when every one of my students failed the test.
16. Sorry, I thought everyone knew about the change of plan.

## 78 / Quiz 2.5.1-2.5.47
1. I worked on my project from noon to midnight.
2. It's a moot point.
3. And then, all of a sudden, her husband burst through the door.
4. Everyone waited with bated breath for the verdict.
5. Do it yourself. I'm not at your beck and call.
6. We were buck naked in the back seat of my car.
7. By and large, the students are pretty clueless.
8. Yesterday's incident is a good case in point.
9. The state that she comes from is chock-full of wackos.
10. You can chalk her win up to hours of training and a bit of luck.
11. I'm champing at the bit to get started on this project.
12. The consensus is that the change was a big mistake.
13. We have some really deep-seated problems in our society.
14. I did a 180 and changed my vote from yes to no on the referendum.
15. Be careful. It's a dog-eat-dog world out there.
16. Every so often, one of my ideas actually works.
17. Someday I'll exact my revenge from that bastard.
18. After Lee surrendered, the Civil War was, for all intents and purposes, over.
19. You'd better hurry. It's first come, first served.
20. It was a sad, heart-rending experience.
21. I couldn't care less what he thinks about me.

22. If worst comes to worst, we can always eat our shoes.
23. We can't afford a new one. We'll just have to make do.
24. I've had it with that guy. I'm going to talk to him man to man and set him straight.
25. The pterodactyl picked me up by my neck.
26. We need to nip this in the bud before it gets any worse.
27. Remember the adage, haste makes waste.
28. I've been on tenterhooks all week waiting for my exam results.
29. Chick peas and garbanzo beans are one and the same.
30. Our company's fiscal year runs from July 1 to June 30.
31. When he talked about Tahiti, it piqued my interest in going there.
32. I can't believe the murderer got off scot-free.
33. He's a shoo-in. He'll win with 90% of the votes.
34. There's going to be a sneak peek of the film before the premier tomorrow.
35. I'm not worried about being indicted. The statute of limitations has expired, so I'm safe.
36. My house is bordered on three sides by the sea.
37. This isn't working. We need to take a different tack.
38. My ex-wife really put me through the wringer.
39. His wife caught them in the throes of passion.
40. Don't pay any attention to him. It's all tongue in cheek.
41. Listen to me. You need to toe the line or get out!
42. Without further ado, here is the star of the show.
43. Talking about my mother's favorite recipes really whet my appetite.
44. The worst-case scenario is that we'll all be eaten by piranhas.
45. That bull really wreaked havoc in my china shop.

## 88 / Quiz 3.1.1-3.1.2
1. I need to see the doctor. This pain is killing me.
2. I haven't seen that movie. I heard it was really good.
3. Carlos went on a diet. He lost 25 lbs.
   Carlos went on a diet, and he lost 25 lbs.
   Carlos went on a diet and lost 25 lbs.
4. We were really tired, so we went to bed.
5. We canceled the picnic because it was cold and rainy.
6. My sister went to a fertility specialist, and she ended up having triplets.
   My sister went to a fertility specialist and ended up having triplets.
7. The movie got great reviews, but it was a huge flop.
   The movie got great reviews but was a huge flop.

## 91 / Quiz 3.2.3-3.2.7
1. The airplane crashed because one of its engines fell off.
2. It's surprising that its roof wasn't torn off by the tornado.
3. My sister's kids rode their bikes to the ice cream shop, but its doors were locked.
4. In Britain, there were four King Georges.
5. The 60s was a tumultuous decade in USA.
6. Yesterday the temperature got down to the low 20s.
7. After three DUIs, he was sentenced to a year in jail.

## 93 / Quiz 3.3.1
1. Please turn handle slowly
2. Snack Bar Will Be Closed Today
3. Employees Must Wash Hands
4. Do Not Block This Way

5. Temporarily Out of Service
6. Restrooms Across the Street

## 95 / Quiz 3.3.2
1. We have a 17-year-old daughter.
2. OK
3. OK
4. Yes, I have a full-time job.
5. OK
6. We live in a five-bedroom house.
7. I have a 35-foot boat.

## 95 / Quiz 3.3.3
1. *And Then There Were None*
2. *Midnight in the Garden of Good and Evil*
3. *So Long, and Thanks for All the Fish*
4. *The Hitchhiker's Guide to the Galaxy*

## 96 / Quiz 3.3.4
1. I watched *Butch Cassidy and the Sundance Kid* last night. It was a great movie.
2. "Billie Jean" was a song on Michael Jackson's album *Thriller*.
3. "Gentlemen of New South Wales" is the title of the tenth chapter of *Fatal Shore*.
4. I'm reading an article named "Lost Tombs of the Pharaohs" in a magazine called *History Revealed*.
5. There was an article titled "The Fury of Forgotten Voters" in today's *Daily Mail* newspaper.

*Also by Carl W. Hart*

**Secrets of Teaching ESL Grammar**
Riverwoods Press, 2015, 2018
ESL grammar teaching advice and methods for novice ESL teachers

**Rocket English Grammar**
Riverwoods Press, 2012, 2018
Basic to advanced English grammar textbook

**Michael Jackson**
Macmillan, 2010
Intermediate level graded reader

**Barack Obama**
Macmillan, 2010
Intermediate level graded reader

**Nelson Mandela**
Macmillan, 2009
Pre-intermediate level graded reader

**Amazing Stories from History**
University of Michigan Press, 2009
Multilevel ELT reading series

**The Ultimate Phrasal Verb Book**
Barron's Educational Series, 1999; 2nd edition, 2009; 3rd edition, 2016; 4th edition, 2020
Definitions, examples, and exercises for 400 common phrasal verbs